Talking Back to Civilization

Indian Voices from the Progressive Era

Related Titles in
THE BEDFORD SERIES IN HISTORY AND CULTURE
Advisory Editors: Natalie Zemon Davis, Princeton University
Ernest R. May, Harvard University
Lynn Hunt, University of California, Los Angeles
David W. Blight, Yale University

THE BEDFORD SERIES IN HISTORY AND CULTURE

Talking Back to Civilization

Indian Voices
from the Progressive Era

Edited with an Introduction by

Frederick E. Hoxie

University of Illinois at Urbana–Champaign

BEDFORD/ST. MARTIN'S   Boston   ♦   New York

For Bedford/St. Martin's

Executive Editor for History: Katherine E. Kurzman
Developmental Editor: Gretchen Boger
Editorial Assistant: Jamie Farrell
Senior Production Supervisor: Joe Ford
Marketing Manager: Jenna Bookin Barry
Project Management: Books By Design, Inc.
Text Design: Claire Seng-Niemoeller
Indexer: Books By Design, Inc.
Cover Design: Zenobia Rivetna
*Cover Art: Blackfoot Indians Talking with Dr. Dixon at Flag Raising Ceremony,
    September 13, 1913, Blackfoot Reservation, Browning, Montana.* Photographer:
    Dr. Joseph K. Dixon, Indiana University Museum, Bloomington, IN.
Composition: Stratford Publishing Services
Printing and Binding: Haddon Craftsmen, an R. R. Donnelley & Sons Company

President: Charles H. Christensen
Editorial Director: Joan E. Feinberg
Director of Marketing: Karen R. Melton
Director of Editing, Design, and Production: Marcia Cohen
Manager, Publishing Services: Emily Berleth

Library of Congress Control Number: 00-105738

Copyright © 2001 by Bedford/St. Martin's

Manufactured in the United States of America.

6
f e d c

For information, write: Bedford/St. Martin's, 75 Arlington Street, Boston, MA 02116
(617-399-4000)

ISBN: 0-312-10385-9 (paperback)
       0-312-12808-8 (hardcover)

Foreword

The Bedford Series in History and Culture is designed so that readers can study the past as historians do.

The historian's first task is finding the evidence. Documents, letters, memoirs, interviews, pictures, movies, novels, or poems can provide facts and clues. Then the historian questions and compares the sources. There is more to do than in a courtroom, for hearsay evidence is welcome, and the historian is usually looking for answers beyond act and motive. Different views of an event may be as important as a single verdict. How a story is told may yield as much information as what it says.

Along the way the historian seeks help from other historians and perhaps from specialists in other disciplines. Finally, it is time to write, to decide on an interpretation and how to arrange the evidence for readers.

Each book in this series contains an important historical document or group of documents, each document a witness from the past and open to interpretation in different ways. The documents are combined with some element of historical narrative—an introduction or a biographical essay, for example—that provides students with an analysis of the primary source material and important background information about the world in which it was produced.

Each book in the series focuses on a specific topic within a specific historical period. Each provides a basis for lively thought and discussion about several aspects of the topic and the historian's role. Each is short enough (and inexpensive enough) to be a reasonable one-week assignment in a college course. Whether as classroom or personal reading, each book in the series provides firsthand experience of the challenge—and fun—of discovering, recreating, and interpreting the past.

Natalie Zemon Davis
Ernest R. May
Lynn Hunt
David W. Blight

Preface

Of all the myths that distort our understanding of the Native American experience, none is more powerful than the belief that the rise of the modern United States caused the destruction of the Indians' culture. At the end of the nineteenth century, the story goes, American expansion eradicated the Indians, defining them forever as people of the past. This story is reinforced by powerful artistic imagery: statues of defeated horsemen, paintings of warriors riding into the sunset, handicrafts marketed as authentic artifacts of a lost world.

Like many myths, the story of the vanishing Indian is rooted in fact. The nineteenth century was a century of dispossession. Native Americans were systematically separated from their homelands in successive waves of warfare and legal maneuvering. American troops forced entire tribes to leave their homes at gunpoint. Settlers murdered their Indian neighbors with impunity. Virulent new diseases killed those who tarried or were weak. For Natives who survived, well-meaning "friends" came forward to force new clothes and new habits on them, to snatch their children away, and to preach disobedience to community elders and healers. By 1890, as a consequence of these actions, the U.S. Census Bureau could count fewer than 300,000 Native Americans in the United States. That figure represented less than half the indigenous population that had inhabited the same area a century earlier and perhaps one-tenth of the number who had been there in 1492.

From the distance of the twenty-first century, however, we can see that these numbers represent something other than the end of Native American culture. If one continues to track the census reports, for example, one finds that the Indian population stabilized in 1900 and slowly began to rise thereafter. By the end of the twentieth century, the Native American community in the United States had expanded seven times over and stood at more than 2 million. Tracing the movements of tribal communities in the twentieth century, one finds that thousands of Indian emigrants moved to towns and cities across the

United States. These adventurers often encountered other Native people with whom they formed new families and neighborhoods that were often defined by innovative forms of work, recreation, and worship. Such social change also brought Indians into regular contact with new institutions: schools, courts, art museums, publishing houses, and newspapers. While those institutions were typically dominated by non-Indians, contact with them inspired Indians to explore new forms of communication and cultural expression, including books, paintings, lawsuits, and perceptive commentaries on contemporary issues.

Through such means, Indians began to talk back to American society. By talking back to those who considered themselves superior, Indians could show that they rejected the self-serving nationalism they heard from missionaries and bureaucrats. The Natives made it clear that they refused to accept the definitions others had of them — savage, backward, doomed. And they attacked people who thought white culture epitomized the virtues of "civilization." The documents collected here capture a cross section of this Indian "back talk" in all of its moods: angry, clever, subtle, tenacious, even playful.

The myth of the vanishing Indian, then, rests on the erroneous belief that Native American history somehow ended at the close of the nineteenth century. By extending our field of vision from 1890 to the present, we can begin to understand that as tragic as the nineteenth century was, it marked but a moment in the long history of a people. Certainly the expansion of the United States destroyed peoples and traditions that can never be retrieved, but that process fell short of wiping out the continent's indigenous cultures. The goal of this book is to help students understand how American Indians in the first decades of the twentieth century inspired the cultural survival that has become the central theme of their modern history.

Talking back to the American public and its leaders usually meant being able to express oneself in English. As a consequence, none of the documents included here presents a critique in a tribal tongue. Not surprisingly, the majority of the statements come from men and women who belonged to the first generation to be educated in the government's extensive network of boarding schools. These were people who had been exposed to the teachings of civilization and were therefore adept at picking out its flaws. The most important source for these examples of talking back to American civilization is the *Quarterly Journal* of the Society of American Indians, an organization of educated Native Americans, founded in 1911, that lobbied for Indian citizenship and improved education. Essays in magazines and books and testimony from congressional hearings are also included in this collection.

While the English-speaking graduates of government schools pioneered the process of talking back to the American public, they were certainly not alone. Tribal leaders had criticized the white man's pretensions in North America from the sixteenth century onward. The educated Indian activists who published their complaints were therefore supported by tribal and reservation leaders whose audiences were smaller but no less perceptive about the shortcomings of civilization. A sampling of those local voices also appear in this volume.

This book opens with an introduction that describes the world Native Americans inhabited in the first decades of the twentieth century and traces the ways in which this community encountered and responded to life in the United States. The introduction provides a historical context for six successive chapters that present American Indian commentaries on various aspects of modern civilization. The first chapter, containing Simon Pokagon's speech delivered at the World's Columbian Exhibition in Chicago in 1893, is followed by five thematic chapters that present critical views of education, Christianity, Indian policy, popular culture, and World War I. A final chapter reprints testimony by reservation leaders before congressional investigating committees in the early 1920s, while the afterword, which includes a petition drafted by a group of Southwestern leaders in 1922, suggests how the talking back of two decades earlier could form the basis for community action.

Each chapter begins with a historical introduction that identifies the authors of the documents and explains the events under discussion. Together with the introduction, these headnotes should make the materials in the book easily accessible to students with no background in Native American history. A chronology of major events during the time period covered by the documents (1890–1928) follows the afterword, as do some suggested questions for discussion and a selected bibliography.

ACKNOWLEDGMENTS

I began this book two jobs ago, so its publication owes a great deal to the patience and support of others. Charles Christensen and Katherine Kurzman of Bedford/St. Martin's have been extraordinarily patient. When they suggested a simpler project several years ago, I assured them this one could be done just as quickly. I was wrong, but they were good natured. I am also grateful to Gretchen Boger, who oversaw the editing of the final volume with great skill and tact. Emily Berleth saw the manuscript through production into its final form with expertise and grace, and Nancy Benjamin provided superb copyediting for this relatively short but complicated text. The illustrations for this volume owe a great deal to the generosity and speed of several outstanding archivists and librarians. Among them are Thomas Kavanagh, curator of the Mathers Museum at Indiana University; Magdalene Moccasin, archivist at the Little Big Horn College Archives; and George Miles of the Beinecke Rare Book and Manuscript Library at Yale University. Most of the research for the volume was carried out at the Newberry Library. As ever, I am grateful to my friends and colleagues there for continuing that institution's tradition of extraordinary service. In particular, I wish to acknowledge the assistance of Robert Karrow, Curator of Special Collections, associate librarian Mary Wyly, photographer John Powell, and JoEllen Dickie of Special Collections. Ayer Reference Librarian John Aubrey provided more than assistance; he is a colleague who gives both help and advice. Both were needed for this project. I am grateful as well to Michael Sherfy, who hunted and gathered with great skill at a crucial stage in the project. I wish to thank as well those friends who helped me clarify my ideas for this book—Elliot Gorn, James Grossman, and Helen Hornbeck Tanner—and the readers who helped me shape and improve the manuscript itself—Colin Calloway, Brenda Child, R. David Edmunds, Peter Iverson, and Sherry Smith. Finally, I wish to acknowledge and thank my students and colleagues at the University of Illinois at Urbana–Champaign. The former have helped me think through the meaning of the documents reprinted here, while the latter have provided a stimulating intellectual home where I could finally pull them all together between two covers.

Frederick E. Hoxie

Contents

Illustrations

Introduction:
American Indian Activism in the
Progressive Era

Charles Eastman, called Ohiyesa by his Santee Sioux kinsmen, lived a life that seemed to bridge the ancient and modern worlds. He was born in 1858 in an isolated, Dakota-speaking village in northern Minnesota beyond the reach of white settlers and missionaries, but he came of age in a bustling world of railroads and telephones. During his childhood the Dakotas occasionally encountered American traders and military men (his mother's father was soldier-artist Seth Eastman), but Eastman grew up in an Indian world in which non-Indian visitors were a rarity. Because his mother died when he was an infant, Eastman was raised by his grandparents. In 1862 his family fled to Canada to escape retaliatory raids triggered by the Minnesota "Sioux uprising." A decade later he was brought back to the United States by relatives who had converted to Christianity. He was enrolled in mission schools and taken up by well-meaning Christians who tried to "save" him for civilization. In addition to teaching him the tenets of Christianity, the missionaries pressed him to speak English, to wear proper Victorian clothes, and to model his life after theirs. He should give up hunting in favor of farming, a skilled trade, or a profession. They believed that he—like other "civilized" people—should live in a log house, marry only one woman, and raise a family.

Eastman's treatment at the Dakota mission schools was typical of the time. In the last decades of the nineteenth century, as the United States government extended its authority over the last Native groups beyond its control, American political and intellectual leaders became convinced that the time had come to end all conflicts with Native Americans by somehow converting them to "civilization." These leaders' impulse rested on their belief that the gulf between American Indian communities and their own Victorian society was deep and unbridgeable. Indians were "backward" peoples; white Americans were "civilized." While Indi-

1

ans had always been viewed by policymakers as culturally deficient, the events of the late nineteenth century gave this language of "civilization" new power. The United States was the world's largest and oldest democracy and was rapidly becoming its largest, most dynamic economy. It seemed self-evident that this rapidly expanding nation was the epitome of "civilization." It took only the smallest of steps in logic to describe the differences between Indians and United States citizens as those between "savagery" and "civilization." The chauvinism and hubris embedded in this triumphant American nationalism offered only one alternative to young men like Ohiyesa: leave your Dakota lifeways behind and take on the habits of American "civilization."

By 1887, when Eastman was twenty-nine, it seemed that his Christian teachers had succeeded. In the spring of that year he graduated from Dartmouth College and prepared to enter Boston University's medical school. He would not marry for another few years, but he had become a Christian; like other "civilized" gentlemen of his day, he wore a stiff white collar and a necktie. As Eastman prepared to move on to a medical career, it seemed he had absorbed the "civilization" that had so completely enveloped his life. He seemed the perfect example of the American Indian who had given up the old, backward life for the new, civilized one. However, a deeper look at the Santee physician's life tells us otherwise.

Thirty years after his Dartmouth graduation, Charles Eastman, M.D., published his autobiography. Containing few of the optimistic platitudes he had been taught in mission school, it dwelled repeatedly on the ideals and beauty of the traditional Sioux culture that he had left behind in the north woods. Eastman noted bluntly that he wasn't so sure the Indian and white worlds could be divided along the lines of savagery and civilization. He had seen supposedly civilized people acting as savages: "The pages of history are full of licensed murder and the plundering of weaker and less developed peoples.... Behind the material and intellectual splendor of our civilization, primitive savagery and cruelty and lust hold sway." Dakota culture, he observed, contained virtues that would endure in the face of recent events. "I am an Indian," he declared, "and while I have learned much from civilization ... I have never lost my Indian sense of right and justice."[1]

In these deeply felt phrases, Charles Eastman was talking back to civilization. A member of a generation of Native people who came of

[1]Charles Eastman, *From the Deep Woods to Civilization: Chapters in the Autobiography of an Indian* (Lincoln: University of Nebraska Press, 1977), 194–95. Originally published in 1916.

age in the post–Civil War era, when American industrial might raced toward a new zenith, he witnessed violent assaults on tribal enclaves across the West. While Eastman was still a young man, professional hunters exterminated the last of the buffalo herds on the Great Plains, politicians dismembered the tribal homelands of Indian Territory, industrial fishing outfits eradicated the traditional lifeways of the Northwest Coast communities, lumberjacks destroyed the virgin pine forests of the north woods, and teams of immigrant laborers laid railroad tracks across the deserts and arroyos of the Southwest. As Eastman and his American Indian contemporaries faced the advent of the twentieth century, they confronted an encroaching American nation in every arena of their lives.

Although they were impressed by America's power, and even persuaded that the United States represented a triumph of civilization, Eastman and his contemporaries were well aware of its faults. During the first decades of the twentieth century, they frequently commented on the way modern society coldly cast aside those who did not conform to its needs. They questioned the values of a society that could create great abundance but was unable to devise a way of distributing its bounty so as to provide for all of its members. Observing the industrial world as outsiders, Eastman and other Native Americans were largely immune to the nation's boosterism and self-satisfaction. And so they talked back. They spoke out at celebrations and nationalistic commemorations. They criticized the actions of the Indian Office and its authoritarian bureaucrats. They proposed alternatives to the government's boarding schools and to its regimented programs for bringing Indians to "civilization." And they poked fun at self-righteous preachers, moralistic politicians, and ignorant citizens who seemed so ready to instruct the Indians on the finer points of civilization. In the process, Native writers like Charles Eastman began to consider the differences between their heritage and the cultures of non-Indians. They identified similarities in the values and desires of different tribes, and they came to see terrible gaps separating those tribes from the ideals of the American majority. They began to define "Indian culture" as an alternative to American civilization and to combine the defense of Native cultures with criticism of modern life. As they talked back to the civilization that had surrounded them, they began to include defenses of Indian cultures as part of their argument.

When he graduated from medical school, Charles Eastman went to work as a physician for the Indian Office, the division of the U.S. Department of the Interior responsible for the government's handling of Indian affairs. He was immediately posted to the Pine Ridge agency in western South Dakota, arriving just in time to witness the rise of an Indian cultural revival called the Ghost Dance and the local officials' overreaction to it. In the fall of 1890, just a few months after Eastman had arrived, the Pine Ridge agent called for troops to stop the spread of the dance. On December 29 the escalating tension between dancers and the Army reached a climax when the Seventh Cavalry opened fire on a band of surrendering ghost dancers near Wounded Knee creek, not far from agency headquarters. More than two hundred people—mostly women and children—were killed that day. Dr. Eastman was called from his Pine Ridge agency office to tend the survivors. Both the massacre itself and the corruption of the Indian Office that had contributed to it eventually drove Eastman from his post. He opened a private practice in Minneapolis but later drifted back to Indian affairs. He served as a field representative for the YMCA and lobbied Congress on behalf of various Sioux legal claims before shifting to writing and lecturing. He was most active politically after 1911, when he joined with other educated Indians to found the Society of American Indians, a reform organization based in Washington, D.C. Although increasingly disillusioned with politics, Eastman continued to speak out into the 1920s. In 1911 he served with W. E. B. Du Bois as a delegate to the Universal Race Congress in London.

The people who joined Charles Eastman during the Progressive Era and talked back to American civilization knew they could not recreate a world peopled only by Indians. They believed military resistance to national "progress" no longer made sense. Nevertheless, they refused to capitulate to the attitudes and pieties of their non-Indian countrymen or to the Indian Office programs that sought to "uplift" them. Rather than embrace the idea that tribal communities could return to the past or accept the invitation to abandon their heritage and take on the trappings of American civilization, Eastman and his contemporaries defined a middle position between those extremes. They believed indigenous values and traditions gave them the strength to resist federal policies and restore the confidence of Native people in their cultures without retreating to the past. And as it embarked on this middle path, Eastman's generation learned that Indians shared a number of complaints in common. Eventually their criticisms helped them see elements in Indian culture around which they all might rally.

Like many of their non-Indian contemporaries who shared their concerns about modern, industrial society, Eastman and his colleagues talked back to American civilization both to challenge its smug presumptions and to ameliorate the brutal impact it had had on its victims. In the process they articulated a vision of Native American culture that inspired persistence in Indian communities across the nation while laying the foundations for cultural revivals that would take place in ensuing decades. By talking back to civilization, Eastman's generation helped define, preserve, and even stimulate faith in "Indianness" for the remainder of the twentieth century.

INDIAN AMERICA, 1900

Prior to Charles Eastman's birth in 1858, most Indian people lived beyond the reach of railroads and well-traveled highways. Even though tens of thousands of their forbearers had died during the previous three centuries in their struggles to resist the European invasion, North American Indians living in the pre–Civil War American West encountered non-Indians infrequently. The two groups met episodically in war, at trading posts, or in council. Prior to 1800, relatively little sustained contact between or social integration of the two societies had taken place.[2] At the turn of the nineteenth century, the five million Europeans living in North America were clustered along the Atlantic Seaboard and in the St. Lawrence and Rio Grande valleys, while most of the 600,000 Indians who had survived the colonial era sustained a separate existence in population centers in other regions of the continent: the Great Lakes, the Southeast, the Plains, the Northwest Coast, and the Southwest. They lived out their everyday lives in communities that were overwhelmingly Indian in population and character.[3]

As Charles Eastman grew to manhood, national expansion obliterated the physical distance separating Native America and the areas of European settlement. Between 1850 and 1900 the principal conflicts of the first half of the century—the forced removals of Native Americans from the Great Lakes region and the Southeast—were replicated in virtually every corner of the country. The U.S. population doubled nearly every twenty years between 1800 and 1900, while the number of indigenous people declined steadily. By the start of the twentieth

[2]The well-known examples of integration such as the Puritan "praying towns" and the intermarriage that occurred among Southeastern tribes such as the Cherokee affected a tiny percentage of the Native American population.

[3]Russell Thornton, *American Indian Holocaust and Survival: A Population History since 1492* (Norman: University of Oklahoma Press, 1987), 90.

century, the Bureau of the Census reported that the United States contained 76,000,000 non-Indians and only 250,000 Indians.[4] These statistics alone paint the outlines of a tragic historical narrative, but even they fail to articulate the fervor with which Euro-Americans pursued the goal of "settling" Native lands or to describe the destruction caused by that process.

The events of the nineteenth century swept forward in a series of violent cycles. Following the forced removals that emptied most of the lands east of the Mississippi of significant Indian populations, it was clear the federal government would not protect native communities from the ambitions of rapidly developing states. Just as Indian Office officials stood aside in the 1830s to allow Georgia and Indiana to evict the bulk of their native populations, they did little in the 1850s to interfere with Californians, Oregonians, and Kansans who elbowed local tribes to tiny reservations while they "settled" their new states.

The 1860s, the decade of the Civil War, brought forth both new dreams of national unity (symbolized in the West by the transcontinental rail project) and new levels of organized violence. Efforts to unite the nation cast resisting tribes in the role of America's enemies, while large-scale military operations (often made possible by the technological and organizational advances of the Civil War) devastated tribes in the Dakotas, Colorado, and Arizona. Massacres such as those at Sand Creek, Colorado, and along the Washita River in Indian Territory, and removals such as the Navajos' forced "Long Walk" from their southwestern homes to the prison camp at Bosque Redondo, New Mexico, punctuated the decade of the 1860s.

During the 1870s and 1880s, smaller conflicts repeated this theme of displacement and subjugation. Despite occasional Indian victories such as occurred at the Little Big Horn in 1876, tribe after tribe — from the Nez Percés of Idaho; to the Apaches of Arizona; to the Comanches, Kiowas, Lakotas, and Cheyennes of the Plains — were confined and separated, and then surrounded by the settlers who poured in around them.

These tragedies drove home the power of American civilization and the Indians' desperate need to devise a strategy for survival. In the 1880s and 1890s, just as thoughtful government officials in Congress

[4]These crude figures obscure the fact that the nineteenth century was also a century marked by the intermarriage of Indians and whites and the rise of a large, non-Anglo-Saxon minority. One should keep in mind that 250,000 was the figure given for the number of people classified as "Indian" by the U.S. Bureau of the Census; the 76,000,000 figure included millions of African and Asian Americans as well as an even larger number of immigrants from Italy, Greece, and other countries in southern and eastern Europe.

and the Indian Office pondered how to provide for the future of Native people, so tribal leaders and the growing number of educated men and women like Charles Eastman began searching for ways to maintain their communities and to build a future for themselves and their families. As they embarked on this search, however, they discovered they faced formidable opposition. They confronted poverty and powerlessness, as well as non-Indians' deeply held beliefs about the nature of Native American culture.

THE "ANTITHESIS OF CIVILIZATION"

At the end of the nineteenth century, faith in American civilization pervaded every corner of national life. Even the usually critical academic world absorbed the rhetoric of national progress. Nowhere was this rhetoric more in evidence than in the historical and scientific writings about Native American culture and history that appeared in the century's final decades. Early in the nineteenth century, the study of American Indian life had been carried out by amateur scholars who were curious about the race's ancient origins and concerned with recording the external appearance and behavior of contemporary tribal groups. These part-time researchers were not especially interested in larger theories of "civilization" and expansion. Most famous of the early investigators were Thomas Jefferson, who excavated a prehistoric earthwork near his Virginia home, and Albert Gallatin, the "father of American ethnology," who devoted his time to compiling vocabularies of native languages. The goal of men like Gallatin and Jefferson was to present "Indian" attributes and beliefs to the public, not to reconstruct Native grammars or elucidate Native philosophies. While confident of the superiority of European civilization, Gallatin, Jefferson, and their kin did not link their studies explicitly to a celebration of American power.[5]

[5]Robert E. Bieder, *Science Encounters The Indian, 1820–1880: The Early Years of American Ethnology* (Norman: University of Oklahoma Press, 1986), 205. For a more recent view of Jefferson, see Anthony F. C. Wallace, *Jefferson and the Indians: The Tragic Fact of the First Americans* (Cambridge: Harvard University Press, 1999), especially chapter 5.

A similar pattern was evident among the artists of the early nineteenth century. With the prominent exception of George Catlin, who published his notebooks in 1844, most painters produced accurate renderings of Native people and their possessions but paid little attention to tribal traditions and beliefs. Charles Bird King and Karl Bodmer, the Swiss illustrator who accompanied Prince Maximilian up the Missouri River in 1833, were typical of this trend. Other students of Indian life recorded physical characteristics (including cranial capacity) and folklore, but prior to midcentury there was little interest in understanding the perspective of living Native communities on history or recent events.

At mid-century, as the pace of westward migration accelerated, scholars and collectors widened their efforts to understand the workings of native communities. The publication of Lewis Henry Morgan's *League of the Ho De No Sau Nee* in 1851 (the first account of an Indian community's traditions based on extensive interviews with tribal members), marked the beginning of this change, as did the opening of the Smithsonian Institution's first exhibits building in 1858. Despite the fact that only one of the Smithsonian's original fifteen display cases contained American Indian materials, the collecting of native artifacts quickly became an institutional priority.

The Smithsonian's ethnological collection grew from 550 items in 1860 to more than 13,000 by 1873. The growth of these collections reflected a shift in the tone of research from amateur cataloguing to systematic study. During the remaining decades of the nineteenth century, the enthusiasm for collecting spread to other museums. Public displays of American Indian life became the basis for programs at Harvard University's Peabody Museum of Anthropology and Archaeology (founded in 1866), the American Museum of Natural History in New York (which opened in 1869), and Chicago's Field Museum of Natural History (opened in the aftermath of the World Columbian Exposition in 1893). These new institutions organized scientific expeditions that competed with one another to collect Native American artifacts and establish research programs in a wide array of specialized areas such as language, kinship, ritual practice, and religion.[6] During the 1890s, research on Native Americans spread to the graduate anthropology departments in the nation's new research universities. This shift marked a major step in Indianist scholarship's move away from the realm of dedicated amateurs and into an arena dominated by university-trained professionals.[7]

The 1902 meeting of the European-based International Congress of Americanists (the first gathering of this European-based group ever held in the United States) symbolized the extent to which twentieth-century scholarly thinking about Indian culture came to be dominated by the mutually reinforcing themes of national expansion and professional scientific ambition. Morris K. Jesup, a New York banker who was one of the American Museum of Natural History's leading benefactors, welcomed the congress to New York by declaring that Amer-

[6]See Douglas Cole, *Captured Heritage: The Scramble for Northwest Coast Artifacts* (Seattle: University of Washington Press, 1985), 10–12, 50, 165.

[7]See Regna Darnell, ed., *Readings in the History of Anthropology* (New York: Harper and Row, 1974), 6–7 and 420–21.

ica had become "a new nation in science." Jesup observed that modern technology had caused "even the remotest parts" of the world to be "touched and quickened by the genius and courage of the explorer." Americans, he noted, "have not been idle in the great field of discovery . . . No more interesting study can occupy the mind of man of the present day than to know for a certainty how this great land was peopled, and the gradual advancement of the human race, from the far back up to the present."[8] Jesup's excitement regarding the "great field of discovery" reflected the popular assumption that his century's conquest of Indian communities had been but a chapter in "the advancement of the human race." For Jesup and his audience, the discovery of native traditions and beliefs could be understood as a feature of a historical process "from the far back up to the present." As historian Curtis Hinsley has written, "the museum process constructed a meaning of Indian demise within the teleology of manifest destiny." By the end of the nineteenth century, Indian cultures had become, in Hinsley's phrase, "dehistoricized," and Indian people transformed into exotics who were the antithesis of "civilization."[9]

American Indians of Charles Eastman's generation confronted both a vastly different set of circumstances than their parents had experienced and an overpowering intellectual orthodoxy that confined them to the margins of both American history and contemporary society. This orthodoxy fueled the government's efforts to dismantle tribal communities and transform Native Americans into "civilized" Americans. In the late nineteenth century, schools for Indians and programs to promote farming among tribes were more than government programs; they were expressions of a uniform conviction that Native American culture had no place in the modern world.

One chilling illustration of the contempt government officials felt for Indian people is a letter written in 1887 by a school teacher working at the Crow Indian reservation in Montana. The agency school was like dozens of others in which Native children were separated from their families, dressed in "citizens' clothes," and provided with a grammar school education in English. But perhaps most disturbing to modern observers was the philosophy that underlay the institution. This philosophy is revealed candidly in the following letter to Indian

[8]*Proceedings of the International Congress of Americanists, 13th Session* (Easton, Penn.: Eachenbach Printing, 1905), xx.

[9]Curtis M. Hinsley, "Zunis and Brahmins," in *Romantic Motives: Essays on Anthropological Sensibility,* ed. George W. Stocking, Jr. (Madison: University of Wisconsin Press, 1989), 170.

Office headquarters in Washington, D.C. In it the teacher proposed a
device for further separating Indian children from the influence of
their parents:

> There should be a board fence 12 feet high, enclosing a space 200
> by 300 yards around the school buildings. There is now only a wire
> fence around the school yard, which is not over 50 feet from the
> front of the school buildings. Every Indian from the camp who
> wishes to, can converse with the pupils, and it cannot be prevented.
> The scenes of camp life, which are weekly presented to their view,
> are very detrimental to the pupils, and the camp gossip, which can
> not now be shut out, is a serious evil to them. With such a (board)
> fence they can be separated almost entirely from the demoralizing
> influences of the camp, and their progress towards civilization will
> be correspondingly accelerated.[10]

A proposal to wall a group of Indian children off from their parents for
the purpose of accelerating their "progress towards civilization" illustrates vividly the governing conviction that Native life and American
life were completely incompatible. Government bureaucrats, scientists, and missionaries alike inhabited a world that supported this ide-
ology and sought to confine Native people to a prescribed "place" in
both American thought and American society.

The same year the Montana teacher called for an impenetrable
fence around his school, Congress approved a general allotment law
sponsored by Massachusetts Senator Henry Dawes. Known as the
Dawes Act, the new statute created a process for placing Native Americans on 160-acre farms carved from their reservation homelands,
beginning the process of forcibly dismantling reservations and extending individual citizenship to tribal members. Employing the industrial
imagery of the day, Amherst College president Merrill E. Gates (a
prominent advocate of policy reform) described the Dawes Act as "a
mighty pulverizing engine for breaking up the tribal mass."[11] Gates
and his well-meaning allies believed that allotment would "pulverize"
the tribal homelands and transform American Indians into owners of
family farms who would emulate the habits of their white neighbors.
They believed the allotment process would accomplish on a grand
scale the kind of conversion missionary teachers had carried out with

[10]H. M. Beadle, Superintendent of the Crow Boarding School, to General H. E.
Williamson, August 20, 1887, in U.S. Commissioner of Indian Affairs, *Annual Report*
(Washington, D.C.: Government Printing Office, 1887), 137.
[11]Francis Paul Prucha, *The Great Father* (Lincoln: University of Nebraska Press,
1984): 671.

individuals like Charles Eastman. As American power spread across Native communities, Indian families would not only be incorporated into the United States, but converted in the process to "civilized" life.

Charles Eastman's declaration that "I am an Indian" was a rejoinder to the confident predictions of scientists like Morris Jesup and reformers like Henry Dawes and Merrill Gates. It was one of dozens of statements published during the Santee Sioux author's lifetime that reminded readers that a dissenting, Native perspective on American history existed and would continue. These statements, in which Native American men and women talked back to the civilization that now enveloped them, appeared in many places. Some Indian authors wrote popular books and magazine articles intended for an American public that, while supporting national expansion, remained curious about Indians. Others spoke out at congressional hearings, during investigations of Indian affairs, or from the columns of the nation's newspapers.

THE PROGRESSIVE ERA

Eastman and his colleagues found an audience for their ideas because they spoke out at a time of American self-criticism and reform. Despite the nation's impressive economic achievements during the last quarter of the nineteenth century, a growing body of Americans had become disturbed by the costs of the nation's new wealth and international prestige. Farmers protested that despite the unprecedented growth in output brought about by the settlement of the West, the massive deployment of mechanical cultivators and threshers, and the rise of such processing centers as Minneapolis, Omaha, and Dallas, agricultural income remained stagnant or was falling. Thousands of credit-starved farmers railed against high transportation costs and unstable prices. Their discontent fueled more than a decade of political insurgency, as traditional politicians such as presidential candidate William McKinley vied with newcomers from the People's party (commonly called the Populist party), the Farmers' Alliance, and other groups for the allegiance of rural voters. While farmers' complaints against banks, railroads, and implement manufacturers played a major role in the politics of the 1890s, the arrival of the new century brought anti-industrial protests from the country to the city.

The growth of American industry in the late nineteenth century was reflected in the sprawling manufacturing centers fueled by coal and an expanding grid of electricity that produced trainloads of new products for the new economy. The output of these manufacturing centers moved swiftly over steel rails to commercial and individual customers across the country and overseas; their movements were routinely managed and coordinated by telegraph and telephone communication. But this system of industrial production was not always efficient or popular. Municipal transportation systems had often fallen into the hands of monopolists who cared little for the public welfare. Their lines often served them more effectively than they served their customers. High tariffs stopped manufactured goods from finding markets in other countries. Collusion among businesses squeezed out competitors and replaced a concern for innovation with greed. And this new empire of commerce depended on thousands of workers who angrily sought recognition for their unions and a living wage for their families.

Farmers and industrial workers were not alone in their unhappiness. Many of the people who had benefited most from the new industrial order—middle-class managers, small businesspeople, and urban professionals—decried the "heartlessness" and indifference of the modern industrial landscape. They and their allies in the press (the original investigative journalists, often called "muckrakers") called on local legislatures, Congress, and the courts to institute reforms that would make their cities more livable, their institutions more accessible, and enterprise more accountable to public needs.

At the turn of the century, a disparate group of men and women emerged from these groups—farmers, industrial workers, and urban activists—to demand action. They called themselves Progressives, and their period of influence (roughly from 1890 to 1920) came to be known as the Progressive Era. During this period, the United States Constitution, which had not been altered for more than thirty years, was amended four times to allow for a graduated income tax, the direct election of senators, women's suffrage, and Prohibition. (Many believed the latter reform would "clean up" the nation's cities and towns.) The movement celebrated a number of heroes. Among these were social worker Jane Addams, who founded the first American settlement house in a Chicago slum in 1889, and President Theodore Roosevelt, who enforced antitrust laws against large industrial combinations, doubled the size of the national parks, and strengthened the regulation of railroads and the food and drug industries. As the Progressive agenda shifted from the Republican party to the Democratic party, Woodrow Wilson's administration extended its reforms to banking regulation and tariff reduction. However, it also led the nation into World War I—a "war to end all wars" inspired by idealism, which eventually exhausted itself. By the 1920s, the fervor for change had subsided and the Progressive Era was over.

Concerned primarily with economic and political reform, the Progressives of the early twentieth century did not focus much of their attention on racial justice. Progressive heroes such as Theodore Roosevelt and Woodrow Wilson accepted the disfranchisement of African Americans in the South and generally embraced the doctrine of white supremacy. The prohibition of Chinese immigration, which had been enacted in 1882, continued through this period and was supplemented by new restrictions on Japanese immigration and land ownership. Despite the presence of the leaders of many European immigrant communities in the Progressive movement, the period also witnessed a rising resentment of "new" migrants from southern and eastern Europe. These newcomers were frequently condemned as members of "backward" races who could not be assimilated into the American melting pot. Those condemnations bore fruit in 1924 when new legislation virtually ended immigration to the United States from anywhere other than northern Europe.

In their calls for new regulations and fair treatment for industrialization's victims, the Native Americans who criticized government policies and anti-Indian attitudes in the Progressive Era echoed many of the non-Indian reformers, but their concerns rarely captured the attention of a broad public. Indians, after all, were a tiny minority of the American population and their concern for racial justice was generally out of step with the progressives' priorities. As a result Native American leaders had few opportunities to publish their opinions. None of the era's "yellow press" publishers or enterprising social scientists displayed a serious interest in Indian affairs, so few Native American authors gained access to the columns of progressive magazines and newspapers. The Indian reformers' principal outlet was the *Quarterly Journal,* published in Washington, D.C., by the Society of American Indians. Between its founding in 1913 and its merger and disappearance in the early 1920s, the *Journal* provided regular commentaries on events that concerned Native Americans. Most of the magazine's writers were educated Indians who, like progressive reformers elsewhere, sought to humanize and democratize life for the benefit of their community. Writers for the *Journal* commented on policy issues but they also addressed broad, cultural concerns: education, religion, and racial stereotypes.

Many of the documents collected in this volume come from the *Quarterly Journal.* They offer opinions on a wide range of subjects that concerned American Indian progressives in the two decades prior to World War I. Excerpts from the *Quarterly Journal* are supplemented by other writings by Native Americans during this generation. These are taken from book and magazine articles published by Indian writers, congressional hearings where tribal leaders took the opportunity to express themselves on public events, and speeches by Native Americans that were reprinted in government reports or in the popular press. Together these statements document the struggle on the part of Indian leaders during the Progressive Era to correct flaws in policy and to reform the public's thinking about both Native cultures and Euro-American civilization.

INDIAN WRITERS RESPOND

American Indian popular writers from the Progressive Era spoke with surprising unity. Charles Eastman, who was probably the best known of these Native authors, wrote an initial autobiographical sketch, *Indian Boyhood,* in 1902; it was published by Boston's Little, Brown and Company. He followed *Boyhood* with nine other books that were published in the East; they described aspects of Native life for a general audience. In all of them the Santee author cast himself in the role of the traditional storyteller—someone who both described the old ways and gave them a personal interpretation. As he wrote in *The Soul of an Indian* (1911), "My little book does not pretend to be a scientific treatise. . . . So much that has been written by strangers of our ancient faith and worship treats it chiefly as a matter of curiosity. I should like to emphasize its universal quality, its personal appeal."[12] Eastman's other books carried out this objective. They included *Old Indian Days* (1907), *Indian Child Life* (1913), and *Indian Scout Talks* (1914).

Interest in Indian folklore, together with the rise of the Boy Scouts and other outdoor-oriented organizations, supported a growing market for books like Eastman's. Christine Quintasket (1884?–1936), a Colville woman who published under the name of Mourning Dove, wrote a novel, *Co-Ge-We-A* (1927) and compiled an anthology of tribal

[12]Quoted in David Reed Miller, "Charles Alexander Eastman, Santee Sioux, 1858–1939," *American Indian Intellectuals,* ed. Margot Liberty (St. Paul: West Publishing, 1978), 64.

tales entitled *Coyote Stories* (1933). She was a contemporary of the Santee author, as were Zitkala Ša (Gertrude Bonnin) (1876–1938), a Yankton Sioux who published two collections of short stories, *Old Indian Legends* (1901) and *American Indian Stories* (1921), and Luther Standing Bear (1868?–1939), who wrote during the 1920s and 1930s. Standing Bear, a Lakota Sioux, produced four books: *My People the Sioux* (1928), *My Indian Boyhood* (1931), *Land of the Spotted Eagle* (1934), and *Stories of the Sioux* (1934). These writers presented themselves not as disinterested scholars but rather as advocates of Indian culture who believed that their indigenous heritage was equivalent to modern "civilization" and that they should be considered fellow human beings rather than members of a "savage" race. "These legends are relics of our country's once virgin soil," Zitkala Ša wrote in 1901, adding that they provided evidence of "our near kinship with the rest of humanity and [point] a steady finger toward the great brotherhood of mankind."[13]

Native American popular writers also peppered their stories with judgments on contemporary American life. Sometimes such appraisals were implied, as authors wrote nostalgically of the Indian past, but authors often made their criticisms explicit. Zitkala Ša's essay "Why I Am a Pagan," which appears in this volume, contrasts a lifeless Indian convert to Christianity with the narrator, who avoids church services to enjoy a beautiful spring day. In the story, the convert can do nothing but "mouth most strangely the jangling phrases of a bigoted creed," while the narrator takes "excursions into the natural gardens where the voice of the Great Spirit is heard in the twittering of birds, the rippling of mighty waters and the sweet breathing of flowers." She declares, "If this is paganism, then at present, at least, I am a pagan."[14] In a passage from his *From the Deep Woods to Civilization,* also included in this volume, Charles Eastman puts his criticism of Christianity into the mouth of a tribal elder whom he quotes as stating, "I have come to the conclusion that this Jesus was an Indian. He was opposed to material acquirement and to great possessions. He was inclined to peace. . . . These are not the principles on which the white man has founded his civilization."[15]

---

[13]Zitkala Ša, *Old Indian Legends* (1901; reprint, Lincoln: University of Nebraska Press, 1985), vi.

[14]Gertrude Bonnin, "Why I Am a Pagan," *Atlantic Monthly* (1901).

[15]Eastman, *From the Deep Woods,* 143.

INDIAN ANTHROPOLOGISTS

Another group of Native writers who both celebrated their own communities' pasts and offered critiques of modern American civilization was made up of individuals who worked with anthropologists and museum collectors to record tribal histories and preserve examples of indigenous artistic expression. These native ethnographers actively promoted the idea that American Indian cultures were more than relics of a backward and disposable past. Their descriptions of the beauty and intricacy of tribal traditions provided an implicit critique of efforts to "pulverize" Native communities into oblivion, offering tribal leaders the ammunition they needed to respond to assertions of Indian "backwardness."

Anthropological "informants" ranged from community members such as George Hunt, who worked with Columbia professor Franz Boas among the Kwakiutl, and James Carpenter, who guided Robert Lowie among the Crow, to the Omaha scholar Francis La Flesche and the Lakota elder Black Elk.[16] After growing to adulthood among the Omaha in the 1870s, La Flesche moved to Washington, D.C., where he became Smithsonian anthropologist Alice Fletcher's partner in an impressive series of ethnographic monographs. Black Elk traveled to Europe with Buffalo Bill in the 1880s and returned to his reservation in midlife because he saw no place for himself in the non-Indian world. On the reservation he worked first as a Catholic catechist and later as a teacher of traditional Lakota rituals and ideas to non-Indian authors.

These native anthropologists understood that by documenting their cultures they were ensuring the cultures' permanence and giving them meaning in the "civilized" world. Franz Boas told a group of Kwakiutl chiefs at Fort Rupert in 1897 that his informant, George Hunt, "would become the storage box of your laws and your stories."[17] Similarly, Black Elk responded to John Neihardt's request for an interview because he believed that the poet's retelling of his life and great vision would preserve a part of Lakota culture. "What I know was given to me for men and it is true and it is beautiful," Black Elk told

[16]See John G. Neihardt, *Black Elk Speaks* (New York: William Morrow, 1932).

[17]Cole, *Captured Heritage,* 158. Boas's student, Robert Lowie, wrote with remarkable parochialism that his mentor "stimulated an enormous amount of high-grade recording by Indians." Lowie recognized the important role of Native Americans in the early years of modern anthropology, but he failed to see that Indian colleagues would share the anthropologist's desire to record ancient lifeways. Robert H. Lowie, *The History of Anthropological Theory* (London: George G. Harrap, 1937), 133.

Neihardt. "You were sent to save it. . . . I can teach you."[18] Anthropologist Margot Liberty's comment about Francis La Flesche's work is relevant to all of these efforts. She observed that he worked "at a time during which old restraints and restrictions upon the divulging of sacred traditions becomes—in the stark awareness of impending cultural loss—pitted against the value of preserving something at least for posterity."[19]

Collaborating with outsiders opened informants up to charges of treason and opportunism, but it also made it possible for white students like Alice Fletcher, Franz Boas, Robert Lowie, and John Neihardt to grasp the richness and complexity of North America's indigenous traditions. The partnership of Native and non-Native scholars gave the Indian scholars access to a sympathetic audience while it won tribal communities a cadre of outsiders who appreciated the depth and scale of their traditional cultures. Many who studied with these Indian ethnographers later made pledges to their partners that were similar to Franz Boas's declaration to a group of chiefs at Fort Rupert: "Wherever I can, I speak for you."[20] When a native scholar spoke in conjunction with a non-Indian scholar, together they pursued a similar goal.

[18]Quoted in Raymond J. DeMallie, ed., *The Sixth Grandfather: Black Elk's Teachings Given to John G. Neihardt* (Lincoln: University of Nebraska Press, 1984), 28. Black Elk's intentions appear clear despite the controversy that continues over the value of both his recitations and Neihardt's version of these, published as *Black Elk Speaks* (New York: William Morrow, 1932). For an introduction to the dispute, see G. Thomas Couser, "*Black Elk Speaks* with Forked Tongue," in *Studies in Autobiography,* ed. James Olney (New York: Oxford University Press, 1988), 73–88.

[19]Margot Liberty, "Francis La Flesche, Omaha, 1857–1932," in Liberty, *American Indian Intellectuals* 53. It is difficult to summarize dozens of examples of collaboration across North America, such as War Eagle's 1928 invitation to the anthropologist Frank Speck that the two of them write a description of the Delaware Big House ritual, a pivotal tribal event last performed in 1924 and seemingly on the verge of disappearing. War Eagle, whose father was Cherokee and whose mother was Munsee, was a tribal leader who had been born in 1880 and was determined to preserve this aspect of his community's past. See Frank G. Speck, *A Study of the Delaware Indian Big House Ritual: In Native Text Dictated by Witapanoxwe* (Harrisburg: Publications of the Pennsylvania Historical Commission, 1931), 2: 7–21. Another notable collaboration is described in James Mooney, *The Swimmer Manuscript: Cherokee Sacred Formulas and Medicinal Prescriptions,* Smithsonian Institution, Bureau of American Ethnology Bulletin 99, revised, completed, and edited by Frans M. Olbrechts (Washington, D.C.: Government Printing Office, 1932).

[20]Cole, *Captured Heritage,* 159. A disturbing example of collaboration occurred between 1936 and 1941 at Isleta Pueblo, where an educated tribal member secretly made drawings of ceremonies for anthropologist Elsie Clews Parsons. While praised by his employers for his accuracy and commitment to the project, the tribal member, Joe B. Lente, insisted that his identity be kept secret until after his death. See Esther S. Goldfrank, *The Artist of "Isleta Paintings" in Pueblo Society* (Washington, D.C.: Smithsonian Press, 1967).

An important subset of native anthropologists celebrated tribal life by presenting it visually. The Arapho painter Carl Sweezy (1881–1953) used butcher paper and house paints to depict modern reservation life. "The way of the white people . . . seemed unsociable and lonely," Sweezy later recalled, so he created images that celebrated traditional family and religious values and inspired tribal solidarity.[21] In a similar way, Ernest L. Spybuck (1883–1949), a Shawnee, recorded ceremonial and social scenes that took place near his Oklahoma home. Using watercolor, pencil, and ink, Spybuck created paintings in which costumes and dances vibrated with color and meticulous detail. The paintings not only documented the artist's world for a wider, non-Indian audience but, like the critiques of Zitkala Ša and Eastman or the stories of Francis La Flesche, they carried an implicit affirmation of that world into the twentieth century.[22]

In the Southwest, the association of Native American artists and white intellectuals inspired other forms of presentation. Anthropologists led by Edgar L. Hewett began commissioning Pueblo Indian painters to record aspects of their ceremonial life. The most famous of these in New Mexico was Crescenio Martinez of San Ildefonso Pueblo, who completed an entire series of paintings before his untimely death in 1918. At the same time, interest from Anglo artists such as Ernest Blumenschein and Bert Phillips in nearby Taos, and the patronage of collectors like Mary Austin and Alice Corbin Henderson, encouraged Martinez and the men who followed him to show their work to a wider audience. By the early 1920s, Martinez's nephew Awa Tsireh (Alfonso Roybal), at San Ildefonso Pueblo, together with Hopis Fred Kabotie and Otis Polelonema and Quah Ah (Tonita Pena) of Cochiti Pueblo, were exhibiting their work in New York and Chicago. By that time as well, a group of six Kiowa painters (who had been encouraged by a young Bureau of Indian Affairs official in Anadarko, Oklahoma) were also exploding onto the national art scene. In 1928 these six—Monroe Tsa Toke, Stephen Mopope, Spencer Asah, Jack Hokeah, James Archiah, and Bou-ge-te Smokey—enrolled in the University of Oklahoma to study with Professor O. B. Jacobson.

---

[21]Margaret Archuleta and Rennard Strickland, *Shared Visions: Native American Painters and Sculptors in the Twentieth Century* (Phoenix: The Heard Museum, 1991), 5.

[22]Lee A. Callender and Ruth Slivka, *Shawnee Home Life: The Paintings of Ernest Spybuck* (New York: Museum of the American Indian, 1984), 7–10. For a review of the same time period in the history of Canadian Indian art, see Gerald R. McMaster, "Tenuous Lines of Descent: Indian Arts and Crafts of the Reservation Period," *The Canadian Journal of Native Studies,* 9, no. 2 (1989): 205–36.

Figure 1. Ernest Spybuck, *War Dance and Gathering Scene*, ca. 1910.
At the same time that writers like Zitkala Ša and Arthur Parker were using their pens to comment on the state of Indian America, Ernest Spybuck, a self-taught Shawnee artist, was using his paintbrush. Spybuck recorded everyday scenes of Indian life near his Oklahoma home, reminding viewers both then and now of the ongoing vibrancy of Native American community life.
Courtesy, National Museum of the American Indian, Smithsonian Institution (N19694).

The connection brought them rapid fame. The group exhibited at the International Congress of Folk Arts in Prague in 1928, and three years later joined with their Southwestern counterparts and others at the Exposition of Indian Tribal Arts in New York City. The exposition show toured the United States and Europe for two years following its New York appearance.[23] By 1931 the *New York Times* was gushing, "Lo, the poor Indian . . . begins to emerge before our newly opened eyes, as artist. . . . Our problem child . . . is suddenly seen to be, in his own, a kind of genius passing our full comprehension."[24]

DEFENDING TRIBAL RELIGIONS

In the first decades of the twentieth century, Indian religious leaders began turning the table on Christian missionaries by arguing that Native traditional beliefs deserved respect rather than eradication. Most prominent in this new discussion of religion were the defenders of the so-called peyote cult, an increasingly popular set of rituals associated with *Lophophora williamsii,* a hallucinogen traditionally used by Apaches in Texas and Arizona. In the 1890s, the construction of rail lines linking south Texas to the Great Plains enabled religious leaders throughout the West to receive supplies of the peyote plant. In the space of two decades, in tribal communities in Oklahoma, Kansas, Nebraska, and Montana, religious leaders called "road men" combined the ancient peyote rite with elements of Christianity to produce an entirely new form of worship. Adopting some of the techniques of Christian missionaries and taking full advantage of rail and automobile transportation, these road men then spread the new faith. By the turn of the century they had reached sixteen different reservations, and by 1918 they had incorporated themselves as the Native American Church.[25]

Emphasizing the importance of monogamy, sobriety, and hard work, peyote road men won a wide following despite the fact that federal authorities sought to outlaw the use of the peyote plant in church rituals. The new faith had a particular appeal to the educated young

[23]See Dorothy Dunn, *American Indian Painting of the Plains and Southwest* (Albuquerque: University of New Mexico Press, 1968), 188–95, 198–201, 218–40.

[24]*New York Times,* 29 November 1931, sec. 5, 12–13; quoted in Dunn, *American Indian Painting,* 239.

[25]David F. Aberle, *The Peyote Religion among the Navaho,* Viking Fund Publications in Anthropology, no. 42 (New York: Wenner-Gren Foundation, 1966), 17.

men and women who returned from federal boarding schools uncertain about how they might fit into reservation life. "Returned students" such as the Osage leader Fred Lookout, who had attended the Indian Office's famed Carlisle Indian School in Pennsylvania, and the Crow Frank Bethune, who was educated closer to home, were persecuted for their adherence to the sect but were not easily deterred.

Peyote men defended themselves by referring to one of the civics lessons they had been taught in the government's schools. As Comanche leader Quanah Parker declared, "I do not think this legislature should interfere with a man's religion."[26] Following the incorporation of the Native American Church, these leaders argued more pointedly that the American constitutional guarantee of freedom from religious persecution obligated the United States government to protect their worship services from harassment. Their legal standing and English-speaking leadership inspired stubborn resistance to government criticism. "We like church," the Ute peyotist William Wash wrote to Washington. He added, "We want to meet every Sunday and have Church and pray and be good . . . we want to rest on Sunday and then on Monday we want to work and farm."[27] His piety in turn inspired similar defenses of other Indian beliefs and practices. In one of the documents included here, Francis La Flesche and Fred Lookout speak out in defense of the peyote ritual.

POLITICAL PROTESTS AND LEGAL CHALLENGES

Among Charles Eastman's generation of Native people who were educated at government schools were hundreds of men and women who, after graduation, used their new facility with English and their understanding of American institutions to lobby for changes in Indian Office policies or to petition the courts to hear their grievances. By criticizing the actions of the government, using the lessons they had been forced to learn, these Natives turned the table on their tormentors. Through their actions, new Indian political leaders defined a set of "rights" they believed Native Americans should enjoy as citizens of their communi-

[26]Quoted in Omer C. Stewart, *Peyote Religion: A History* (Norman: University of Oklahoma Press, 1987), p. 75.

[27]David Rich Lewis, "Reservation Leadership and the Progressive-Traditional Dichotomy: William Wash and the Northern Utes, 1865–1928," *Ethnohistory,* 38, no. 2 (Spring 1991): 134, 139.

ties and residents (albeit prior to 1924 usually as noncitizens) of the United States.[28] Their outspokenness helped mark the first decades of the twentieth century as the opening round of a new campaign to defend Native American assets and interests in courtrooms and legislative chambers.

Examples abound of returned students talking back to the Indian Office's officious bureaucrats. In northern Wisconsin, for example, Reginald Oshkosh, a graduate of the Carlisle School and the son of Neopit Oshkosh, the Menominee's traditional chief, worked tirelessly to end federal supervision of the tribe's vast timber reserves. Reginald Oshkosh conceded that federally regulated lumbering on the reservation had brought employment to hundreds of his kinsmen, but he believed the government should provide his tribe with more than wage labor. Refusing to take on the role of the backward Indian grateful for federal largesse, Oshkosh declared his tribe's goal was not subsistence but "to become independent and self-supporting and [to] terminate our relations as wards of the Government."[29] Although many leaders disagreed with Oshkosh's call for an end to federal support, his aggressiveness was widely applauded. Across the continent at Fort Yuma, in the southwestern corner of Arizona, another Carlisle student became active in tribal affairs and carried on his interest even after he was sent to the Pennsylvania school. In 1899, Patrick Miguel, son of a Quechan leader whom the government insisted on calling "ex-Chief Miguel," wrote the local agent from his dormitory room, warning him "not to touch the Indians again" or he would be reported to the Indian Office. Upon his return to Yuma a decade later, the young man continued to advocate tribal self-government. Urging the Indian commissioner to authorize elections at the agency, he echoed Oshkosh's refusal to play the role prescribed for him by the government: "We believe the old Indians should be taught more by members of their own tribe, in a kindly way, to see and adopt the white man's laws and it is to this end the more progressive members of the tribe request that they be allowed to have a council and presiding officer to pilot the ship of state of the Yumas." A contemporary of Miguel's at

[28]While Congress declared all Native Americans to be citizens in 1924, many thousands of individuals had been granted citizenship when they took up allotments under the 1887 Dawes Act.
[29]Quoted in Brian C. Hosmer, "Creating Indian Entrepreneurs: Menominees, Neopit Mills, and Timber Exploitation, 1890–1915," *American Indian Culture and Research Journal,* 15, no. 1 (1991): 15.

Fort Duchesne, Utah, declared, "This is our home and we do not want to be disturbed. . . . We do not want to be discouraged."[30]

In Indian Territory, Delos Lone Wolf, the Carlisle-educated nephew of the Kiowa chief Lone Wolf, returned from boarding school to discover that Congress had violated its treaty with the tribe by "opening" new lands for white settlement without first securing the approval of the tribe. Recognizing that the time for speeches and petitions had passed, Delos persuaded his uncle and other leaders to file suit in U.S. District Court seeking an injunction to halt the land sale. Supported by cattlemen who wished to protect their leases on tribal pasture land, Lone Wolf enlisted former Illinois congressman William M. Springer as the tribe's attorney. The ultimate result of his efforts was *Lone Wolf v. Hitchcock,* a 1903 Supreme Court decision that pronounced the congressional abrogation of the Kiowa treaty constitutional. This defeat for Lone Wolf and the Kiowa accelerated the rate of federal seizure of tribal land, but it nonetheless indicated that Indians were willing to do more than talk in the political arena.[31] Congressional testimony from Crow political leader Robert Yellowtail, and representatives of the Ojibwe, Pine Ridge Sioux, and Winnebago tribes are included in this volume.

In the first decades of the twentieth century, most of the Indians' legal activism was focused on the U.S. Court of Claims. The law stipulated that tribes had to gain the approval of Congress for any suit against the United States. Once that approval was secured, however, groups could sue for damages caused by federal action and for payments they had been promised but had not received. In 1881, Choctaws determined to win compensation for lands lost in Mississippi and Alabama a half-century earlier were the first to gain access to the claims process. Their success inspired others. Proceedings in the court of claims were attractive: unlike *Lone Wolf* and other civil suits, claims cases unfolded over a long period of time and carried few

[30]Miguel quoted in Robert L. Bee, *Crosscurrents along the Colorado: The Impact of Government Policy on the Quechan Indians* (Tucson: University of Arizona Press, 1981), 55, 59; quoted in Lewis, "Reservation Leadership," 139. Ironically, Patrick Miguel had been sent to Carlisle as punishment for taking part in the burning down of some boarding school buildings at the Fort Yuman agency. For the successful career of another former Carlisle student, see Terry P. Wilson, "Chief Fred Lookout and the Politics of Osage Oil, 1906–1949," in *Indian Leadership,* ed. Walter L. Williams (Manhattan, Kans.: Sunflower University Press, 1984), 46–53.

[31]William T. Hagan, *United States–Comanche Relations: The Reservation Years* (New Haven: Yale University Press, 1976), 263–65.

immediate risks. By World War I thirty-one claims had been brought to the court.[32] The Winnebago tribe's case for a claim against the United States is made in congressional testimony included in chapter 7 of this volume.

In addition to the emergence of new leaders and the launching of new lawsuits, the first decades of the twentieth century witnessed the emergence of new Indian political pressure groups. These included the Black Hills Treaty Council, which was organized on the Cheyenne River Sioux reservation in South Dakota in 1911 to prepare a suit in the U.S. Court of Claims; the Alaska Native Brotherhood, founded in 1912, and the Alaska Native Sisterhood, founded in 1915; and New Mexico's All-Pueblo Council organized in 1922. The last group emerged from the struggle over land titles between Rio Grande Pueblo communities and non-Indian settlers who had moved onto their lands during the last half of the nineteenth century. The All-Pueblo Council articulated a position common to many other groups when it declared that the Rio Grande communities had lived "in a civilized condition before the white man came to America," and it called on the "American people" to help Indians preserve "everything we hold dear—our lands, our customs, our traditions."[33] The Pueblo leaders' statement, reprinted in this volume, combines an appeal to public morality with pride in their tribal past and is an attempt to turn interest in their culture into political clout. By the end of the 1920s, appeals like this one were winning support from sympathetic non-Indians and enabling tribal leaders to carry on campaigns in every region of the United States.[34]

[32]Unscrupulous attorneys were the frequent target of nervous federal officials. For a broad history of this early claims process, see Harvey D. Rosenthal, "Indian Claims and the American Conscience: A Brief History of the Indian Claims Commission," in *Irredeemable America: The Indians' Estate and Land Claims,* ed. Imre Sutton (Albuquerque: University of New Mexico Press, 1985), 35–71. Statistics on the numbers of cases filed are on p. 40.

[33]*Santa Fe New Mexican,* 6 November 1922, quoted in Willard Rollings, "The Pueblos of New Mexico and the Protection of Their Land and Water Rights," in *Working the Range: Essays on the History of Western Land Management and the Environment,* ed. John R. Wunder (Westport, Conn.: Greenwood Press, 1985), 3–24.

[34]Most of the literature on this period focuses on the decline of the Society of American Indians (SAI) and on the early career of John Collier, the former social worker who founded the American Indian Defense Association in 1923 and became Franklin Roosevelt's commissioner of Indian affairs in 1933. While this focus is reasonable, it has unfortunately diverted scholars from exploring the political dynamics in Native American communities that undermined the SAI's effort to create a unified reform group and, ultimately, made careers like Collier's possible. Preoccupation with these national organizations and figures has also obscured many smaller-scale movements. For example, Native American veterans played an important role in the campaign to win a declaration of universal citizenship for all Indians. Many tribal communities were ambivalent about

TALKING BACK BRINGS RESULTS

The Native American voices raised in the Progressive Era might well have been forgotten had they not been echoed in successive generations and amplified by sympathetic non-Indian allies. In each arena, the pioneering efforts of writers, artists, anthropological informants, religious leaders, lawyers, and politicians established a forum in which American Indian people could discuss the task of sustaining ancient traditions in a hostile and rapidly changing world. Their writings placed America's claim to represent "civilization" under sharp scrutiny while at the same time emphasizing the positive aspects of Native American cultures. These Native efforts affected popular literature, college and university curricula in anthropology and sociology, and legal scholarship that sought to locate the role of tribal governments in the nation's Constitution.

Native American Progressives thus created a tradition for Indian intellectuals who followed the generation of Charles Eastman and Zitkala Ša. In the 1930s and 1940s, writers such as John Joseph Mathews and D'Arcy McNickle, anthropologists such as Ed Dozier, and churchmen Vine Deloria and Francis Frazier expanded on the ideas of their predecessors and developed ties to one another that produced new intertribal organizations, among them the National Congress of American Indians and the National Indian Education Association. Their efforts attracted non-Indian allies to their cause. Indian commissioner John Collier, anthropologist Ruth Benedict, popular writer Oliver La Farge, and legal theorist Felix Cohen are only a few of those who endorsed the idea that tribal cultures should play a central role in modern Indian life.

While Charles Eastman's and others' decisions to talk back to American civilization were eliciting responses, the Native American population was experiencing a stunning growth in population. Beginning

---

citizenship itself, of course, but their experiences in the military encouraged Indian veterans to advocate this form of legal acceptance. Congress declared honorably discharged Native Americans to be citizens in 1919; five years later the status was extended to the entire group. See Russel Lawrence Barsh, "American Indians in the Great War," *Ethnohistory,* 38, no. 3 (Summer 1991): 294–96. For the potency of Indian citizenship and voting, see also Stephen W. Haycox, "Racism, Indians and Territorial Politics," *Alaska History,* 2, no. 1 (Winter 1986): 17–37.

Other regional groups included the Northwest Federation of Indians, which launched efforts to protect the fishing rights of Puget Sound tribes in 1919; the Algonkian Council of Indian Tribes, founded in New England in 1926; and the Four Mothers Society, organized by Redbird Smith and other traditionalist Cherokees in the wake of Oklahoma statehood (which was achieved in 1907).

from a low point of approximately 240,000 in 1890, the total number of American Indians enumerated by the U.S. Bureau of the Census rose gradually during the first half of this century until in 1960 it exceeded 500,000. This growth in numbers ensured that Indian and non-Indian intellectuals would not be speaking in a vacuum; rather, they would be articulating concerns and defining issues in tandem with Native American community leaders and politicians and their white allies. By the time of Charles Eastman's death in 1939, it was clear that his life had formed a bridge to a new world. His tribe and community had suffered greatly at the hands of American settlers, but its future was no longer in doubt.

The Indians who talked back to American civilization in the first decades of the twentieth century established the earliest infrastructure for the modern Native American community. By making their ideas known, finding places where they could be heard, and encouraging the emergence of new political leaders, they made it possible for Indians to communicate with outsiders and with each other in new ways. As the Native population grew in the 1930s and 1940s, there emerged with it a new sense of confidence and optimism that encouraged even greater activism. With this activism came an understanding that artists, politicians, religious leaders, and others shared a common cultural tradition as Native Americans. They came to believe in an Indian with a common political agenda. As these insights were communicated among Indian leaders, a national Native American community began to take shape. Not surprisingly, this new community was—and continues to be—led by popular writers, religious leaders, tribal politicians, anthropologists, and lawyers.

In 1933, Luther Standing Bear wrote that if he had a child to educate, and "was faced with the duty of choosing between the natural way of my forefathers and that of the white man's present civilization," he would "unhesitatingly set that child's feet in the path of my forefathers. I would raise him to be an Indian!"[35] Not only did Standing Bear's statement repeat the now-familiar assertion that Native culture was as legitimate as Euro-American civilization, it also underscored his conviction that Native American peoples shared a common ethnic identity and a common destiny. Asserted in the confined space of an English language book and couched in romantic language that would also appeal to sympathetic whites, the claim "I would raise him to be

---

[35]Luther Standing Bear, *Land of the Spotted Eagle* (Boston: Houghton Mifflin, 1933), 258–59.

an Indian!" stands in striking contrast to Morris Jesup's self-confident observation that Indian cultures were best understood as a minor part of the tableau of progress. Standing Bear's voice and those of others of his generation remind all who hear them how a powerless group can struggle to be heard in a hostile society and, in the course of that struggle, can both form a new version of their identity and alter the world they inhabit.

THE STRUCTURE OF THIS BOOK

This introduction has traced the emergence of different groups of Indian leaders—writers, anthropologists, religious spokespeople, political leaders, lawyers, and artists—in the Progressive Era. The documents contained in this volume are presented according to major subjects these leaders addressed. The introduction should help you understand who these people were; the documents will present what they said.

The first chapter presents a speech delivered by a Potawatomi leader at the 1893 World's Columbian Exposition. Intended as a response to the fair's celebration of the Columbus voyages, Simon Pokagon's "Red Man's Greeting" presents an initial attempt by an Indian leader to criticize the idea that the European settlement of America represented a victory for civilization. Chapter 2 contains commentaries on the keystone of the government's civilization program: Indian education. Excerpts from the *Quarterly Journal* and a chapter from Omaha anthropologist Francis La Flesche's autobiography comment on the government's practice of removing children to government boarding schools and indicate the kind of schooling Indian leaders would have preferred. Chapter 3 shifts the focus to religion. It includes Zitkala Ša's essay "Why I Am a Pagan," defenses of the peyote ritual offered before Congress by La Flesche and Osage leader Fred Lookout, and a chapter from Charles Eastman's *From the Deep Woods to Civilization* titled "Civilization as Preached and Practiced."

Chapter 4 contains three commentaries on federal Indian policy taken from the pages of the *Quarterly Journal*. Reflecting the thinking of the leaders who founded the Society of American Indians, these essays attack the paternalism of the Indian Office and demand a greater role for Native Americans in policy making. Chapter 5 reprints a number of cartoons that appeared in the *Quarterly Journal* and were intended to poke fun at the American public's ignorance of Indian culture and Indian affairs. These images provide a window on the popular attitudes and stereotypes that most disturbed Native American leaders during the Progressive Era. The focus of chapter 6 is World War I, a crusade to "save democracy" to which Indians were recruited despite the fact that they had yet to receive a blanket declaration of American citizenship. The irony of this fact, together with other Native American reflections on the idealism surrounding the war in Europe, is conveyed in three excerpts from the *Quarterly Journal* and a speech given by Crow leader Robert Yellowtail in 1919, while President Woodrow Wilson was in France negotiating the Versailles Treaty that ended the war.

A final chapter illustrates the connection between the commentary of Native American writers and intellectuals and the political concerns of grassroots leaders. It presents testimony given to congressional committees investigating conditions on four reservations. In each case we see tribal leaders struggling with issues that would continue to preoccupy reservation communities for decades to come: legal claims against the United States, questions regarding the legitimacy of tribal governments, Indian Office paternalism, and the conflict between a community's desire to be free of federal control and its need for federal protection. The testimony in chapter 7 makes clear that the Native American leaders whom non-Indians had hoped would promote the "civilization" of their communities had instead turned their attention to advocating tribal interests. Rather than provide evidence for the disappearance of Native communities, this testimony from the 1920s suggests the remarkable extent to which Indian people had adapted to the challenges of the new century.

Together these documents offer us an opportunity to view an era of national growth and overseas triumph from the perspective of Americans who, like Charles Eastman, measured progress according to an indigenous scale. Understanding their perspective should help us broaden our vision of the national past and deepen our view of the American present.

1

Speaking Out at the World's Columbian Exposition, 1893

The Chicago World's Fair, organized to celebrate the four hundredth anniversary of Christopher Columbus's first voyage to America, opened on May 1, 1893. The ceremonies marking that occasion featured speeches by fair organizers and politicians, and began with an American Indian chief stepping forward and tolling a replica of Philadelphia's Liberty Bell. Simon Pokagon, a Potawatomi leader who had been born in 1830 during the presidency of Andrew Jackson, had witnessed the forced removal of most of his tribe and others from the Midwest. Pokagon came from a cluster of largely Catholic Potawatomi villages in southwestern Michigan that had managed to elude federal authorities and maintain their hold on their lands.

Pokagon must have found the invitation to address the American public on so celebrated an occasion both tempting and troubling. After all, he was a survivor of the American onslaught the fair had been organized to celebrate. Born before the founding of the vast city that formed the backdrop for his address, he had personally witnessed—and suffered from—most of the technological "progress" displayed and praised in the exposition's massive exhibit halls: the coming of the railroad, the clearing of the Midwest's forests, the advent of mechanized agriculture, and the spread of large-scale industrial manufacturing. What, indeed, could he say? Whatever discomfort Pokagon might have felt in 1893 would have been at least partially balanced by the fact that much of his community's success in evading eviction from Michigan and surviving the violence of the nineteenth century had resulted from his and his kinsmen's willingness to cooperate with the American authorities. They had embraced Catholicism; they had taken up farming; they had professed loyalty to the national government. The Potawatomi leader could not refuse the invitation to speak in Chicago, but he would be less than honest if he simply joined the general celebration.

Figure 2.   Simon Pokagon.

This photograph of Simon Pokagon was taken about the time he delivered his *Red Man's Greeting* at the Chicago World's Columbian Exposition in 1893.

Courtesy of the Edward E. Ayer Collection, The Newberry Library, Chicago.

Simon Pokagon Offers The Red Man's Greeting
1893

*The product of Pokagon's dilemma was "The Red Man's Greeting," deliv-
ered on the opening day of the fair and sold afterward as a pamphlet. The
text reprinted here is taken from an edition of the speech, which Pokagon
had printed on birchbark, that he and his Chicago lawyer, C. H. Engle,
sold at his lectures and public appearances. It was widely circulated after
the fair and even after Pokagon's death in 1899. While not the only
example of a "civilized" Indian speaking critically of American culture
prior to 1900, it was certainly the most widely disseminated statement of
its kind delivered by a living tribal leader. "The Red Man's Greeting"
reminded its non-Indian readers that America's "civilization" had been
purchased with the defeat of Native people and the disruption and destruction of their lifeways. Surrounded by symbols of American progress
and national pride, Pokagon attempted to turn his hosts' language
against them, to show that "progress" should also include a recognition of
an Indian perspective on events.*

> Shall not one line lament our forest race,
> For you struck out from wild creation's face,
> Freedom—the selfsame freedom you adore,
> Bade us defend our violated shore.

In behalf of my people, the American Indans, I hereby declare to you,
the pale-faced race that has usurped our lands and homes, that we
have no spirit to celebrate with you the great Columbian Fair now
being held in this Chicago city, the wonder of the world.

No; sooner would we hold the high joy day over the graves of our
departed than to celebrate our own funeral, the discovery of America.
And while you who are strangers, and you who live here, bring the
offerings of the handiwork of your own lands and your hearts in admiration rejoice over the beauty and grandeur of this young republic and
you say, "Behold the wonders wrought by our children in this foreign
land," do not forget that this success has been at the sacrifice of *our*
homes and a once happy race.

Simon Pokagon, *The Red Man's Greeting* (Hartford, Mich.: C. H. Engle, 1893).

Where these great Columbian show-buildings stretch skyward, and where stands this "Queen City of the West" *once* stood the red man's wigwams; here met their old men, young men, and maidens; here blazed their council fires. But now the eagle's eye can find no trace of them. Here was the center of their wide-spread hunting grounds; stretching far eastward, and to the great salt Gulf southward, and to the lofty Rocky Mountain chain westward; and all about and beyond the Great Lakes northward roamed vast herds of buffalo that no man could number, while moose, deer, and elk were found from ocean to ocean; pigeons, ducks, and geese in a near bow shot moved in great clouds through the air, while fish swarmed our streams, lakes, and seas close to shore. All were provided by the Great Spirit for our use; we destroyed none except for food and dress; had plenty and were contented and happy.

But alas! The pale faces came by chance to our shores, many times very needy and hungry. We nursed and fed them, fed the ravens that were soon to pluck out our eyes and the eyes of our children; for no sooner had the news reached the Old World that a new continent had been found, peopled with another race of men, than, locust-like, they swarmed on all our coasts; and, like the carrion crows in spring, that in circles wheel and clamor long and loud, and will not cease until they find and feast upon the dead, so these strangers from the East long circuits made, and turkey-like they gobbled in our ears, "Give us gold, give us gold." "Where find you gold? Where find you gold?"

We gave for promises and "geegaws" all the gold we had and showed them where to dig for more; to repay us, they robbed our homes of fathers, mothers, sons, and daughters; some were forced across the sea for slaves in Spain, while multitudes were dragged into the mines to dig for gold, and held in slavery there until all who escaped not, died under the lash of the cruel task-master. It finally passed into their history that, "the red man of the West, unlike the black man of the East, will die before he'll be a slave." Our hearts were crushed by such base ingratitude; and, as the United States has now decreed, "No Chinaman shall land upon our shores," so we then felt that no such barbarians as they, should land on *ours. [The Chinese Exclusion Act, passed in 1882, prohibited Chinese immigration into the United States.]*

In those days that tried our fathers' souls, tradition says, "A crippled, grey-haired sire told his tribe that in the visions of the night he was lifted high above the earth, and in great wonder beheld a vast spider web spread out over the land from the Atlantic Ocean toward the setting sun. Its net-work was made of rods of iron; along its lines in all directions rushed monstrous spiders, greater in strength, and larger far than any beast of earth, clad in brass and stripping in their course the flight of birds that fled before them. Hissing from their nostrils came forth fire and smoke, striking terror to both fowl and beast. The red men hid themselves in fear, or fled away, while the white men trained these monsters for the war path, as warriors for battle."

The old man who saw the vision claimed it meant that the Indian race would surely pass away before the pale-faced strangers. He died a martyr to his belief. Centuries have passed since that time, and we now behold in the vision as in a mirror, the present net-work of railroads, and the monstrous engines with their fire, smoke, and hissing steam, with cars attached, as they go sweeping through the land.

The cyclone of civilization rolled westward; the forests of untold centuries were swept away; streams dried up; lakes fell back from their ancient bounds; and all our fathers once loved to gaze upon was destroyed, defaced, or marred, except the sun, moon, and starry skies above, which the Great Spirit in his wisdom hung beyond their reach.

Still on the storm-cloud rolled, while before its lightening and thunder the beasts of the field and the fowls of the air withered like grass before the flame—were shot for love of power to kill alone, and left to spoil upon the plains. Their bleaching bones now scattered far and near, in shame declare the wanton cruelty of pale-faced men. The storm unsatisfied on land swept our lakes and streams, while before its clouds of hooks, nets, and glistening spears the fish vanished from our waters like the morning dew before the rising sun. Thus our inheritance was cut off, and we were driven and scattered as sheep before the wolves.

Nor was this all. They brought among us fatal diseases our fathers knew not of; our medicine-men tried in vain to check the deadly plague; but they themselves died, and our people fell as fall the leaves before the autumn's blast. To be just, we must acknowledge there were some good men with these strangers who gave their lives for ours, and in great kindness taught us the revealed will of the Great Spirit through his Son Jesus, the mediator between God and man. But while we were being taught to love the Lord our God with all our heart, mind, and strength, and our neighbors as ourselves, and our children were taught to lisp "Our Father who art in heaven, hallowed be thy name," bad men of the same race, whom we thought of the same belief, shocked our faith in the revealed will of the Father, as they came among us with bitter oaths upon their lips, something we had never heard before, and cups of "fire-water" in their hands, something we had never seen before. They pressed the sparkling glasses to our lips and said, "Drink, and you will be happy." We drank thereof, we and our children, but alas! Like the serpent that charms to kill, the drink habit coiled about the heart-strings of its victims, shocking unto death love, honor, manhood—all that makes men good and noble; crushing out all ambition, and leaving naught but a culprit vagabond in the place of a man.

Now as we have been taught to believe that our first parents ate of the forbidden fruit, and fell, so we fully believe that this fire-water is the hard-cider of the white man's devil, made from the fruit of that tree that brought death into the world, and all our woes. The arrow, the scalping knife, and the tomahawk used on the war-path were *merciful* compared with it; *they* were used in our defense, but the accursed drink came like a serpent in the form of a dove. . . .

You say of us that we are treacherous, vindictive, and cruel; in answer to the charge, we declare to all the world with our hands uplifted before high Heaven, that before the white man came among us, we were kind, outspoken, and forgiving. Our real character has been misunderstood because we have resented the breaking of treaties made with the United States, as we honestly understood them. The few of our children who were permitted to attend your schools, in great pride tell us that they read in your own histories, how William Penn, a Quaker, and a good man, made treaties with nineteen tribes of Indians, and that neither he nor they ever broke them; and further, that during seventy years while Pennsylvania was controlled by the Quakers, not a drop of blood was shed nor a war-whoop sounded by our people. Your own historians, and our traditions, show that for nearly two hundred years, different Eastern powers were striving for the mastery in the new world, and that our people were persuaded by the different factions to take the war path, being generally led by white men who had been discharged from prisons for crimes committed in the Old World. . . .

It is clear that for years after the discovery of this country, we stood before the coming strangers as a block of marble before the sculptor, ready to be shaped into a statue of grace and beauty; but in their greed for gold, the block was hacked to pieces and destroyed. Childlike we trusted in them with all our hearts; and as the young nestling while yet blind swallows each morsel given by the parent bird, so we drank in all they said. They showed us the compass that guided them across the trackless deep, and as its needle swung to and fro only resting to the north, we looked upon it as a thing of life from the eternal world. We could not understand the lightning and thunder of their guns, believing they were weapons of the gods; nor could we fathom their wisdom in knowing and telling us the exact time in which the sun or moon should be darkened; hence we looked upon them as divine; we revered them—yes, we trusted in them, as infants trust in the arms of their mothers.

But again and again was our confidence betrayed, until we were compelled to know that greed for gold was all the balance-wheel they had. The remnant of the beasts are now wild and keep beyond the arrow's reach, the fowls fly high in air, the fish hide themselves in deep waters. We have been driven from the homes of our childhood and from the burial places of our kindred and friends, and scattered far westward into desert places, where multitudes have died from homesickness, cold, and hunger, and are suffering and dying still for want of food and blankets.

As the hunted deer close chased all day long, when night comes on, weary and tired, lies down to rest, mourning for companions of the morning herd, all scattered, dead, and gone, so we through weary years have tried to find some place to safely rest. But all in vain! Our throbbing hearts unceasing say, "The hounds are howling on our tracks." Our sad history has been told by weeping parents to their children from generation to generation; and as the fear of the fox in the duckling is hatched, so the wrongs we have suffered are transmitted to our children, and they look upon the white man with distrust as soon as they are born. Hence our worst acts of cruelty should be viewed by all the world with Christian charity, as being but the echo of bad treatment dealt out to us. . . .

We never shall be happy here any more; we gaze into the faces of our little ones, for smiles of infancy to please, and into the faces of our young men and maidens, for joys of youth to cheer advancing age, but alas! instead of smiles of joy we find but looks of sadness there. Then we fully realize in the anguish of our souls that their young and tender hearts, in keenest sympathy with ours, have drunk in the sorrows we have felt, and their sad faces reflect it back to us again. No rainbow of promise spans the dark cloud of our afflictions; no cheering hopes are painted on our midnight sky. We only stand with folded arms and watch and wait to see the future deal with us no better than the past. No cheer of sympathy is given us; but in answer to our complaints we are told the triumphal march of the Eastern race westward is by the unalterable decree of nature, termed by them "the survival of the fittest." And so we stand as upon the seashore, chained hand and foot, while the incoming tide of the great ocean of civilization rises slowly but surely to overwhelm us. . . .

2

Critics of Indian Education

Efforts to "educate" Native Americans away from their traditions and toward the lifeways of Europeans characterized Indian-white relations from the colonial period onward. Using the justification that they wished to teach their captives the splendors of Western civilization, explorers frequently kidnapped young Natives and took them back to England, France, or Spain. Few survived the experience. Squanto was a famous exception to this tradition of one-way journeys. Captured from his home in modern-day Massachusetts and carried off to Europe as a teenager, this resourceful Wampanoag from Cape Cod was unimpressed by what he saw. But he proved adept at using his linguistic skill to persuade his captors that he had seen the light and would be a great help to them if they could transport him back to New England. He returned to his coastal homeland just in time to greet the Pilgrims in perfect colloquial English.

In the seventeenth and eighteenth centuries the colonial societies that began to take shape in North America frequently supported schools and missions designed to "raise up" the Indians to "civilization." While rarely successful, they were popular with mission groups and comforting to government officials who routinely bullied their way onto Indian land and then claimed to be acting in the Indians' best interests. The most famous of these missions were the "praying towns" of eastern Massachusetts in which groups of refugees created Native communities modeled on nearby Puritan villages. There Indians, who had decided to cast their lot with the Christians, settled in villages and lived under the guidance of white ministers. While Indian in many aspects of their social life and subsistence patterns, these communities provided temporary shelter for families displaced by the European advance. Similar towns formed in western Massachusetts, New York, and Ohio during the eighteenth century, but most were swept away in the wake of large-scale settlement and subsequent warfare. King Philip's War brought about the end of the praying towns; a century later, the border conflicts with the French in Canada, the Revolutionary War against the British, and the American settlement of Ohio destroyed most of the others.

During the nineteenth century, federal authorities took over Indian education from the missionaries. The American government's interest was usually greatest during periods of geographical expansion. Thus Congress took the unprecedented (and probably unconstitutional) step of approving subsidies for Christian missionary-teachers during the prosperous aftermath of the War of 1812; after that initiative the establishment of agency schools emerged as a routine fixture of the removal treaties that cleared eastern tribes from the path of an expanding agricultural empire. By the time of the Civil War, the Indian Office had begun to argue that tribal enclaves—now called reservations—should contain federally subsidized institutions that would offer Native residents a common school education. Educated Indians would be peaceful Indians, the bureaucrats reasoned, and therefore would be unlikely to oppose American settlement. This vision of peaceful cultural change bore fruit in the 1870s and 1880s, when the Office of Indian Affairs, sometimes run by men experienced as school administrators, created its Division of Indian Education and established large, off-reservation boarding schools in every region of the country. The most prominent commissioner of this era was Thomas Jefferson Morgan, a former college president who established a uniform curriculum for the Indian school system during the administration of President Benjamin Harrison.

At a minimum, Indian parents were skeptical of the white man's educational programs. Ben Franklin related the story that Canassatego, an Oneida chief, once told him that the Indians who attended the white man's schools were "absolutely good for nothing." As American expansion gathered steam, however, few tribal leaders could joke about the choices being placed before them. In the late nineteenth century, as the Indian educational system became more embedded in the federal bureaucracy, the Natives' situation grew more coercive. School attendance became mandatory and government officials grew increasingly efficient at locating truant children and placing them in school. Once enrolled, children absorbed lessons prepared for them by the Indian Office. Nearly every moment of their lives was programmed and scrutinized to ensure that they would not "retreat" to the ways of their parents. Parents who might see the value of learning English and other basic skills were horrified by the schools' authoritarian routines. Indian agents and policemen arrested children who did not appear in school, and discipline became a central feature of the education that took place in individual classrooms. Even worse from an Indian parent's perspective, the off-reservation boarding schools, including the famous Carlisle Indian Industrial School established in Pennsylvania in 1879, usually organized themselves along military lines. Arriving students would receive severe haircuts, wool uniforms, and instruction in close-order drill. Military-style bands would play while students marched to class and to meals under the watchful eye of headmasters who frequently modeled themselves after Carlisle's founder, Captain Richard Henry Pratt. The benefits of education—literacy, a skilled trade, knowledge of the American governmental system—came only to the students who were lucky or hardy enough to survive this grim routine.

Despite the dislocations and hardships accompanying instruction in the white man's ways, tribal leaders were quick to see the benefits of literacy in English and familiarity with American society. When able to control the instructors, tribes were often eager to have schools established in their communities. Samson Occum, a Mohegan Indian who converted to Christianity, established Christian schools among the Oneidas and at his new settlement of Brothertown, New York, in the late eighteenth century. In the nineteenth century, the Cherokees employed both Native and white schoolmasters to extend literacy throughout their communities and to establish a comprehensive school system in the post-removal homeland of Oklahoma. Other tribes followed suit.

By the end of the nineteenth century, American Indian leaders saw clearly the dilemma that education presented. On the one hand, training in English, mathematics, and other disciplines was essential for success in the industrial world they saw taking shape around them. Few besides tribal religious leaders believed the Native American future would not require an extensive program of education and vocational training. On the other hand, the education most commonly available to Indians was offered by arrogant government officials who expected Indian communities to conform to Victorian social standards and, ultimately, to vanish. Not only did this pessimistic outlook encourage bleak, authoritarian classroom methods, but it also justified an emphasis on vocational training. Leaders interested in preparing their children for community leadership had difficulty recommending the government's schools with their lessons in plowing, dishwashing, and berry picking.

The four documents in this section reflect the ambivalence Native Americans felt toward education in the first decades of the twentieth century. Written by educated Indians, they naturally convey the sense that the lessons taught in schools could be useful to Native people. They indicate their authors agreed with white officials that traditional lifeways needed to be transformed by the schools. At the same time, these documents acknowledge the tragedies and dislocations caused by the current educational system. The writers seem caught between their allegiance to the virtues of education and their loyalty to their fellow Indians. Together, these four statements provide a glimpse of a group of early-twentieth-century Native Americans who struggled to define an approach to Indian education that acknowledged the value of schooling while articulating the specifically Native American community interests it might serve. Rather than speaking out directly about the schools, these authors asked, "How can Indians be schooled without being regimented, degraded, and alienated from their families? How can education serve *Indian* interests?"

Francis La Flesche on Boarding School
1900

The first document is from one of the earliest published memoirs of a boarding school graduate. Published in 1900, The Middle Five: Indian Schoolboys of the Omaha Tribe *was a nostalgic portrait of a student's experiences at the Presbyterian mission school on the Omaha reservation. Its author, Francis La Flesche (1855/62?–1932), speaks in the voice of an educated easterner, but he describes his childhood along the banks of the Missouri River with considerable affection. He wrote the book while living in Washington, D.C., where he had moved in the 1880s to assist anthropologist Alice Cunningham Fletcher in her research. Adopted by Fletcher as her son, La Flesche spent the rest of his adult life working both alone and in tandem with his "mother" to record the histories and cultural practices of his own and other North American Indian tribes. On the surface,* The Middle Five *appeared to be a series of Tom Sawyer–like tales of classroom high jinks in which a group of friends, calling themselves the "Middle Five" gradually mature while they adapt to a new environment. A member of a prominent Omaha trader family*

Francis La Flesche, *The Middle Five: Indian Schoolboys from the Omaha Tribe* (Boston: Small, Maynard, 1900), xvi–xvii, xviii–xix, 3–12, 96–100.

Figure 3.   Francis La Flesche with His Half-Sister, Susette La Flesche, 1879.

Francis and Susette La Flesche in 1879, the year the two of them toured the East with Ponca chief Standing Bear. La Flesche was about twenty when this picture was taken, and Susette was about twenty-five. She was a teacher at the government school on the Omaha reservation. Soon after the tour, Francis began his forty-year friendship and collaboration with anthropologist Alice Cunningham Fletcher.
Nebraska State Historical Society.

of mixed French and Indian ancestry, La Flesche appeared to write without an explicit political agenda. His goal, he wrote in the book's introduction, was "to reveal the true nature and character of the Indian boy."

But in the introduction to his book, La Flesche observed that revealing an Indian's "true nature" was not a simple task. White people harbored serious prejudices against Indians, he noted, and Native people remained suspicious of their adversary's motives and behavior. School children, he asserted, would be the best vehicle for creating a more positive image. By presenting his subjects in clean uniforms and with short hair, the author hoped he would overcome his readers' prejudices. La Flesche's "reasonable" approach was also an indirect way to have his readers acknowledge at the outset the persistence of negative Indian stereotypes. As the author explained, "The paint, feathers, robes and other articles that make up the dress of the Indian . . . are marks of savagery to the European. . . . So while the school uniform did not change those who wore it . . . it may help these little Indians be judged . . . by what they say and do."

La Flesche's reminder that the subjects of the story are Indians — whose uniforms do not change who they are — subtly alters the tone of his memoir. The children he describes are rebelling against adult authority, but they are also acting against the authority of the United States and the forces of "civilization." La Flesche invites his readers to identify and sympathize with the schoolchildren in his book, and by doing so he also invites readers to recognize the humanity of Indian children like himself who were the focus of so much federal effort. One is meant to ask, "Why was this educational system created? Would non-Indian children be treated this way?" The document does not talk back directly to its readers or to government authorities, but its friendly tone and appealing structure create sympathy for the pupils in the boarding school and cause us to question the distance that supposedly separates the "uncivilized" children and the "civilized" teachers in the narrative.

Preface

. . . Among my earliest recollections are the instructions wherein we were taught respect and courtesy toward our elders; to say "thank you" when receiving a gift, or when returning a borrowed article; to use the proper and conventional term of relationship when speaking to another; and never to address any one by his personal name; we were also forbidden to pass in front of persons sitting in the tent [traditional tribal lodge] without first asking permission; and we were strictly enjoined never to stare at visitors, particularly at strangers. To us there seemed to be no end to the things we were obliged to do, and to the things we were to refrain from doing.

From the earliest years the Omaha child was trained in the grammatical use of his native tongue. No slip was allowed to pass uncorrected, and as a result there was no child-talk such as obtains among English-speaking children,—the only difference between the speech of old and young was in the pronunciation of words which the infant often failed to utter correctly, but this difficulty was soon overcome, and a boy of ten or twelve was apt to speak as good Omaha as a man of mature years.

Like the grown folk, we youngsters were fond of companionship and talking. In making our game sticks and in our play, we chattered incessantly of the things that occupied our minds, and we thought it a hardship when we were obliged to speak in low tones while older people were engaged in conversation. When we entered the Mission School, we experienced a greater hardship, for there we encountered a rule that prohibited the use of our own language, which rule was rigidly enforced with a hickory rod, so that the new-comer, however socially inclined, was obliged to go about like a little dummy until he had learned to express himself in English.

All the boys in our school were given English names, because their Indian names were difficult for the teachers to pronounce. Besides, the aboriginal names were considered by the missionaries as heathenish, and therefore should be obliterated. No less heathenish in their origin were the English substitutes, but the loss of their original meaning and significance through long usage had rendered them fit to continue as appellations for civilized folk. And so, in place of Tae-noo'-ga-wa-zhe, came Philip Sheridan; in that of Wa-pah'-dae, Ulysses S. Grant; that of Koo'-we-he-ge-ra, Alexander, and so on. Our sponsors went even further back in history, and thus we had our David and Jonathan, Gideon and Isaac, and, with the flood of these new names, came Noah. It made little difference to us that we had to learn the significance of one more word as applied to ourselves, when the task before us was to make our way through an entire strange language. So we learned to call each other by our English names, and continued to do so even after we left school and had grown to manhood....

... Oddities of speech, profanity, localisms, and slang were unknown in the Omaha language, so when such expressions fell upon the ears of these lads they innocently learned and used them without the slightest suspicion that there could be bad as well as good English.

The misconception of Indian life and character so common among the white people has been largely due to an ignorance of the Indian's language, of his mode of thought, his beliefs, his ideals, and his native institutions. Every aspect of the Indian and his manner of life has always been strange to the white man, and this strangeness has been magnified by the mists of prejudice and the conflict of interests between the two races. While these in time may disappear, no native American can ever cease to regret that the utterances of his father have been constantly belittled when put into English, that their thoughts have frequently been travestied and their native dignity obscured. The average interpreter has generally picked up his knowledge of English in a random fashion, for very few have ever had the advantage of a thorough education, and all have had to deal with the difficulties that attend the translator. The beauty and picturesqueness, and euphonious playfulness, or the gravity of diction which I have heard among my own people, and other tribes as well, are all but impossible to be given literally in English. . . .

The Mission

Leaning against the wall of a large stone building, with moccasined feet dangling from a high wooden bench on the front porch, sat a little boy crying. His buckskin suit, prettily fringed and embroidered with porcupine quills of the brightest colors, indicated the care bestowed upon him by fond parents. Boys and girls were at play around the house, making the place ring with their merry laughter as they chased each other among the trees, but the little boy sat all alone, sobbing as though his heart would break. A big boy came and sat by his side, put his arm around him, and in a kindly tone said, in Indian:

"What are you crying for? Don't cry — I'll play with you and be your friend. I won't let the boys hurt you."

"I want my mother! I want to go home!" was all the homesick little chap could say, crying harder than ever.

"You will see your mother soon, we can go home every bathing-day (Saturday). It is only three days to wait, so don't cry. I have to go away, but I will be back soon. Play with this dog until I come" — putting into the hands of the little boy a wooden dog.

A bell rang, and from every direction came boys and girls crowding and pushing one another as they entered two of the large doors of the building. The big boy came running, and, grasping the little one by the hand, fairly dragged him along, saying: "Come, quick! We are going to eat."

They entered a large room filled with people. Parallel to the walls stood tables of great length, at one end of which the two boys took seats. After considerable hard breathing and shuffling by the children, they suddenly became very still, everyone bowed his head, then a man with gray hair and whiskers, who sat at the end of one of the tables, spoke in a low tone. He finished speaking, then followed a deafening clatter of a hundred tin plates and cups. Young women carrying great pans of steaming food moved rapidly from table to table. One of these girls came to the two boys, and put into the plate of the younger a potato. "Give him two, he's hungry," whispered the big boy to the girl.

Everything was strange to the little new-comer and he kept looking all around. The lamps that were fastened to the walls and posts, the large clock that stood ticking gloomily on a shelf, and the cupboard with its tin door perforated in a queer design were objects upon which his eyes rested with wonder.

The supper over, the boys and girls who sat on the inner side of the tables turned to face the center of the room, and folded their arms. Then they all sang. When this was done, they dropped on their knees and the gray-haired man began to talk again. The little boy watched him for a while, then laid his head on the hard bench,—the tones of the old man grew fainter and fainter until the boy lost all consciousness of them. Suddenly there burst upon him a noise like thunder. He arose to his feet with a start, and, bewildered, he looked around. Everything seemed to be in a whirl. He took fright, ran to the door that first caught his sight, and went with a thud down to a landing, but did not lose his balance; he took another step, then fell headlong into a dreadful dark place. He screamed at the top of his voice, frightened almost into a fit. A woman picked him up and carried him in her arms up a flight of stairs, speaking to him in a language that he could not understand.

This was my first experience at the boarding school established by the Presbyterian Board of Foreign Missions for the instruction of the children of the Omaha tribe of Indians.

The mission school, the founding of which had marked an epoch in the tribe, was located among the wooded bluffs of the Missouri on the eastern part of the reservation. The principal building was of stone, plain and substantial, and plastered inside and out. It was three stories high and had an attic. This attic was perhaps the most interesting part of the structure, for we boys were quite sure it was tenanted by ghosts, and that the devil, who figured considerably in the instruction given us, had full sway in this apartment.

There was a large square hole close to the head of the stairs that led up to the attic. This hole had the greatest terror for us; there was a constant whistling within it, and out of it came sounds like distressing moans and sighs. I remember once, when Gray-beard had sent me up to the attic for something, that I never hurried so on any other errand as I did on that one. I found the article he desired, put it under my arm, and cautiously approached the head of the stair, keeping an eye on the dark hold, then suddenly I made a dash past it, and with amazing rapidity thundered downstairs. "Lad, you will break your neck!" exclaimed Gray-beard. I told him I liked to run downstairs!

Under the attic was the boys' dormitory. The beds were placed close together, and some were wide enough for three boys. The room was large, and in the middle of it stood a post. I have reason to remember this, for one night I got up in my sleep and ran with all my might against this post, making such a noise as to awaken Gray-beard and the superintendent, who came up in great haste with candles in their hands. I was laid up for days after this exploit, but I never ran in my sleep again.

Beneath our dormitory were the parlor and the bedroom of Gray-beard, our teacher and disciplinarian. This name was not inherited by him, nor was it one of his own choosing; the boys gave it to him because his beard was iron-gray, and the Indians adopted it from the boys. In his room at night he might have heard strange noises from the cherubs in the dormitory above, in fact he came up there quite often, rod in hand, as a reminder that such sounds made sleep impossible.

Under Gray-beard's rooms was the school-room where we struggled with arithmetic, geography, history, and A B C, up to the Fifth Reader. This room corresponded in size to our dormitory, but it had no middle post.

The dining-hall, where on my arrival I had taken fright and stampeded head foremost into the cellar, was in the middle of the first story. It was very large and held, beside the three long tables, a big stove in the middle between two large posts. I remember these posts very well, I kept close company with one of them, on my return from a run-away expedition. . . .

The rooms on the two stories above the dining-hall were occupied, one as a play-room for the girls, the others by the various employees.

On the same floor with the school-room and the dining-hall, at the north end of the building, was the chapel. Here we sat in rows on Sunday mornings, afternoons, and evenings, and on Thursday evenings, ranged on long, high wooden benches without backs, our feet scarcely touching the floor, and listened (sometimes) to sermons which were remarkable for their length and sleep-enticing effects. I had many delightful dreams in this chapel, about Samson and his jaw-bone war club, and the fight between David and Goliath, and the adventures of Joseph the dreamer,—stories that were the delight of my boyhood. Brush, one of my dearest friends at the school, knowing my weakness, secured a seat back of mine on purpose to support me when I was in a slumberous mood. I shall never forget his goodness; he now sleeps in the cemetery just above the Mission.

The two large rooms over the chapel were occupied by our superintendent and minister. Above his apartments was the girls' dormitory, while over all stretched the haunted, ghostly attic.

There were other buildings grouped around: to the back stood the store-house and the smoke-house; out of the later came our delicious hams and our sermons, for a part of this building was used as the minister's study. Then there was the great barn where we boys played hide-and-seek in the hay-mow; the corn-crib with its yellow wealth showing between the boards; and the dusty wheat-bins with padlocked doors. Below on the bottom were the Government saw and grist mills, where we often went to see the grinding of the Indians' grain and the large trees sawed into lumber for Agency use or for the Indians' houses. The carpenter and blacksmith shops were also down there, and a long wooden house for the occupancy of the Government employees. All of these buildings stood for the fulfillment of the solemn promise made by the "Great Father" at Washington to his "Red Children," and as a part of the price paid for thousands and thousands of acres of fine land.

Although there were high hills just back of the school, from which one could get excellent views of the surrounding country, we boys preferred to go up into the belfry on the top of the main building for our observations. We did not go often; two difficulties were in the way: the securing of permission from the superintendent, as but few boys could be trusted up there; and we must go through the haunted attic to get to the belfry. No boy during my school days ever went up there alone.

My friend Brush, being quite a favorite with the superintendent, often had permission to go, and took me with him. When we were once in the belfry, we felt safe from the annoyances of the devil and the other horrible things in the attic. The superintendent, without the asking, let Brush have a big spy-glass, which the other boys were not permitted to use, and with it we could see far beyond the river and the valley that stretched in the distance to the opposite bluffs, that were always nearly hidden in a bluish haze. Bringing the glass to a closer range, we could see below, on our side of the river, the rich fields of the Mission and of the Indians; and we used to watch the Indians and the hired men of the school at work there. Sometimes we caught sight of a steamboat far down the river coming up, trailing a long line of smoke; then, with great excitement, we would run down and tell the boys, and all of us would hasten to the highest point near the school and watch the "mystic boat" as it slowly made its way along the winding stream.

To the south of the Mission, overlooking the Missouri and a small lake, stood the highest hill for miles around. This was known by the Indians as "the hill on which Um'-pa-ton-ga (Big Elk) was buried. He was one of the greatest chiefs of the Omahas.

Before schools of any kind were known among the Omahas, Indian parents warned their boys and girls against a free association with the children of persons who did not bear a good character. "Who was that you were playing with?" a father or mother would ask. "Nobody knows the child's family,—beware of him, do not go with him, he will throw upon you the habit of lying and stealing. Go with children whose parents are respected by the people." Such advice would be given by the reputable men and women of the tribe to their children as to choosing their play-fellows.

At the school we were all thrown together and left to form our own associates. The sons of chiefs and of prominent men went with the sons of the common people, regardless of social standing and character. The only distinction made was against cowardice; the boy who could not fight found it difficult to maintain the respect of his mates, and to get a place among the different "gangs" or groups of associates the boys had established among themselves. I learned this from my friend Brush, to whom I complained one day of being abused by the boys when he was not near. "You must look out for yourself now," he said. "If the boys know you won't fight, they will tease you all the time. You must fight."

So the next boy who rudely shoved me aside and knocked my hat off received a painful surprise, for my right fist came so hard against his cheekbone that he stood for a moment as though stunned. Then he moved, and I moved, and the boys standing near could hardly tell which was which until we separated, pretty well bruised. After that the boys were careful not to knock my hat off my head; if they did, they took pains to let me know that it was not intentional.

I told Brush about this set-to, and he approved of it. "That's right," he said; "fight any of them, even if you know that you're going to get licked; then they won't tease you."

My father was the principal chief of the tribe and leader of the village of the "make-believe white-men"; he had plenty of horses, the standard of Indian wealth, yet that did not entitle me to a place in any of the different "gangs" in the school; I had to show that I was not afraid to stand up and fight. Even good-natured Brush had to bristle up at times and engage in a lively tussle, else there would have been no peace for him. Now I was wanted by the smaller "gangs" and invited by them to their places of sport; but Brush held on to me and kept me out. . . .

A New Study

It was a hot September afternoon; our gingham handkerchiefs, which matched our shirts, were wet with mopping our faces. We all felt cross; Gray-beard was cross, and everything we did went wrong.

Warren, who had been sent to the spring for a pail of cold water, leaned over his desk to Brush, and whispered loud enough for the boys around us to hear, "A big black carriage came up to the gate just now, and the Agent and three other big fat men got out. The superintendent shook hands with them, and they went to his room."

While Gray-beard was shaking a boy to make him read correctly, the news of the black carriage and the fat men went from boy to boy. The girls were dying to know what word it was the boys were passing around; but the aisle that separated them from us was too wide to whisper across. Warren's girl made signs to him which he at first did not understand; when he caught her meaning, he tore a fly-leaf out of his book, wrote on it, rolled it into a ball and threw it to the girl, who deftly caught it; these two were adept at such transmission of messages. The girl unfolded the paper, read it, and passed it on; then the girls felt better and resumed their work.

The class in mental arithmetic took the floor. Not one of the boys knew his lesson. As the recitation went on Gray-beard's face darkened and his forehead wrinkled; he came to a timid youngster with a hard question. I knew there was going to be trouble for the little chap; so, to save him pain and distress, I thought of a plan by which to distract Gray-beard's attention. I reached under my desk and took hold of a thread which I carefully drew until my thumb and finger touched the stiff paper to which it was attached, then as the boy stammered out of the wrong answer and Gray-beard made an impatient movement toward him, I gave the thread a gentle pull, "Biz-z-z-z-z!" it went.

"Who's making that noise?" asked Gray-beard, turning toward our end of the school-room.

I loosened the pressure, and the noise ceased. When Gray-beard returned to the boy, I again pulled the thread, "Biz-z-z-z-z!" Something was wrong this time; the buzzing did not cease, it became louder and angrier.

"Who's doing that?" exclaimed Gray-beard.

Every boy and girl looked up to him as though to say, "I did not do it." The buzzing went on; I alone kept my eyes on my book, and so aroused suspicion. I did not dare to put my hand under the desk again to stop the buzzing for I had lost the thread. Gray-beard came towards me and asked, "What have you there?" I did not answer.

"Stand up and let me see!" he exclaimed. Before I could give him any warning, he put his hand in the desk and felt about; he sprang back with a cry, "Ah! I'm bitten! Is it a snake?"

"No, it isn't," I answered; and peering carefully into the desk, I drew out the buzzing thing and showed it to him; it was only a wasp fastened by its slender waist to a sheet of paper.

Although he felt relieved of his fright, the pain of the sting was arousing his anger, and I saw that there was trouble coming to me; but at that moment the door opened and in walked the superintendent and the four fat men. Gray-beard went forward and was introduced to them. There was a scramble by three of the large boys to get chairs from the dining-room for the visitors. When the gentlemen had made a quiet survey of our faces, they sat down and questioned Gray-beard about the branches taught at the school, and the progress made by the pupils. In the meantime, I had released my prisoner; it went buzzing around the room, and then maneuvered over the bald head of one of the visitors, who beat the air with his hands to ward it off.

"Frank, catch that wasp," said Gray-beard.

I caught the troublesome creature in my hat and turned it out of doors.

When the questioning of the visitors was over, Gray-beard turned to us and said, "Now, children, pay strict attention; these gentlemen want to see what you have learned. I will put some questions to you."

We became so silent that we could hear a pin drop. The visitors smiled upon us pleasantly, as though to encourage us.

"Who discovered America?" asked Gray-beard. Dozens of hands went up. "Abraham, you may answer."

An expression of amusement spread over the faces of the scholars as the great awkward boy stood up. Gray-beard must have been bewildered by the sting of the wasp and the sudden appearance of visitors, else he would not have made such a blunder; for he knew very well what every boy and girl of the school could do; however there was no help for it now; Abraham Lincoln, standing with his hands in his pockets, had the floor; he put his weight on one foot and then on the other, the very picture of embarrassment; he cleared his throat, looking helplessly at me, and then at Brush,—"Come," said Gray-beard, "we are waiting."

"George Washington!" answered Abraham.

A titter ran around among the pupils. Gray-beard's face turned red, then white, as he said, "Abraham, take your seat. Brush, can you tell us who discovered America?"

"Columbus," promptly answered the boy. Then a series of questions were asked, which the children answered voluntarily, and did credit to their teacher. The visitors nodded approvingly to each other. When the examination was over, the Agent arose and, addressing the school, said:

"You have acquitted yourselves well in this sudden and unexpected test; I will now ask you to spell for me. Here is a book," said he, turning the leaves of a pretty gilt-edged volume, "which I will give to the scholar who can spell best."

Taking a spelling book, he gave out the words himself. We all stood up, and those who misspelled a word sat down. One by one the pupils dropped to their seats, until only Brush, a big girl, and I remained on the floor; finally I went down, and the girl and Brush went on; they were now in the midst of the hard words. At last Brush failed; the girl also misspelled the word; but as the prize could not be divided, it was given to her.

"Are the children taught music?" asked one of the strangers.

"No," replied the superintendent; "but they can sing nearly all of the Sunday-school hymns."

"They should be taught music as well as reading and spelling," remarked one of the gentlemen, then, addressing the children, he asked:

"Have your people music, and do they sing?"

"They do," answered one of the large boys.

"I wish you would sing an Indian song for me," continued the man. "I never heard one."

There was some hesitancy, but suddenly a loud clear voice close to me broke into a Victory song; before a bar was sung another voice took up the song from the beginning, as is the custom among the Indians, then the whole school fell in, and we made the room ring. We understood the song, and knew the emotion of which it was the expression. We felt, as we sang, the patriotic thrill of a victorious people who had vanquished their enemies; but the men shook their heads, and one of them said, "That's savage, that's savage! They must be taught music."

So it came about that every afternoon after this visit we spent an hour on a singing lesson. We learned quite a number of songs, but we sang them by ear, as it was difficult for us to understand the written music. . . .

Laura Kellogg Attacks the Government's System of Indian Education

1913

The second document is from a speech delivered to the Society of American Indians (SAI) by Laura (Minnie) Cornelius Kellogg (1880–1949), an Oneida, in 1913. Kellogg was born in 1880 on the Wisconsin reservation occupied by the Oneida tribe, an Iroquois community that had left New York State under threat of eviction in 1822. She was educated at an Episcopal school in nearby Fon du Lac. She attended a number of

Laura Cornelius Kellogg, "Some Facts and Figures on Indian Education," *Quarterly Journal,* 1 (1913): 34–46.

Figure 4.   Laura Cornelius Kellogg.
A member of the Oneida community that had migrated voluntarily from New
York State in the early nineteenth century, Laura Kellogg captured her audiences with her command of Iroquois languages and her moving descriptions
of the Iroquois Confederacy's traditional life. Drawing on her studies at some
of the most prestigious institutions of her day, Kellogg struggled to overcome
her audiences' stereotypical racial views. Like many of her contemporaries,
she was an advocate of universal schooling for Indian youth and of economic
self-sufficiency for reservation communities. She is shown here at the far
right, with a group of Oneida Indian mothers.
Courtesy of the Oneida Nation Museum.

*colleges—Barnard, Columbia, Stanford, Cornell, and the University of
Wisconsin—but she did not receive a degree. Fluent in Mohawk,
Oneida, and English, Kellogg was an outspoken defender of the Iroquois
and maintained a lifelong interest in winning compensation for those
lands that had been lost to American speculators at the end of the American Revolution. In 1911 she was one of the founding members of the
SAI, and her criticism of the Indian Office's educational efforts probably
reflected the view of most members. Kellogg's proposed reforms were more*

controversial. She supported transferring Indian children to local public schools. While many agreed with her criticisms of the government's educational program, most members, particularly people from large but geographically isolated reservation communities, believed there was no alternative to the schools run by Bureau of Indian Affairs. During the 1920s and 1930s, Kellogg's fierce opposition to the Indian Office alienated her from other Indian leaders. She eventually retreated to her Wisconsin home, stirring little notice when she died in 1949. Despite the disagreements surrounding her solutions, Kellogg's attack on the government's patronizing educational programs spoke for a broad constituency.

. . . I have never forgotten the figure for education an Old Nez Percé Chief gave at one Carlisle Commencement. He said, "When I was a boy the old chiefs used to say, as soon as you can climb a high mountain, the highest you can find, do not stop halfway and look back. Climb till you reach the top. There you can breathe deep and look into all the valleys. Then you can say, '*I have seen.*' "

There are old Indians who have never seen the inside of a classroom whom I consider far more educated than the young Indian with his knowledge of Latin and Algebra. There is something behind the superb dignity and composure of the old bringing up; there is something in the discipline of the Red Man which has given him a place in the literature and art of this country, there to remain separate and distinct in his proud active bearing against all time, all change.

When Tecumseh was called to Vincennes, and intrigue and defeat were staring him in the face, in the open council, an aide to General Harrison called him to the General's side by saying, "Your *white father* wishes you to sit beside him." Tecumseh answered, "My father? The sun is my father, the earth is my mother, upon her bosom I will recline," and seated himself with the ease of one who dares to be himself. How different in tone is the expression we too often hear from the government school Indian as an excuse for anything he has done poorly: "Well, I am only an Indian!" I have no patience with this last expression. It isn't characteristic of our ancient pride. . . .

Under the philosophy of pantheism which the American native lived, there was a great regard for natural law. I for one am not certain that the discipline under it is not to be respected just as much as that under the artificial.

It has not been appreciated that the leisure in which the American Indian lived was conducive to much thought and that the agitations and the dangers of the wilderness gave him a life rich in emotions. These combined with his unobscured first principles and the stringent discipline to a high standard of character, really gave him an aesthetic education. His choice, when it is native, and not borrowed, is fine; always the artistic thing in preference to the unattractive practical. He loved the beautiful because he had an educated sense of things. . . .

. . . When we stop to think a little, old Indian training is not to be despised. The general tendency in the average Indian schools is to take away the child's set of Indian notions altogether, and to supplant them with the paleface's. There is no discrimination in that. Why should he not justly know his race's own heroes rather than through false teaching think them wrong? Have they not as much claim to valor as Hercules or Achilles? Now I do not say here that everything he has natively is right or better than the Caucasian's. Not at all, but I do say that there are noble qualities and traits and a set of literary traditions he had which are just as fine and finer, and when he has these, for the sake of keeping a fine spirit of self-respect and pride in himself, let us preserve them. . . .

We live in a country that is young and gloriously admirable in many ways. But the growing heterogeneity of population makes polite culture less appreciated by the masses than it was even in revolutionary days. And where wealth is the ruling power and intellectual attainments secondary, we must watch out as a people that we do not act altogether upon the dictates of a people who have not given sufficient time and thought to our own peculiar problems, and we must cease to be dependent on their estimates of our position. . . .

Until we ourselves . . . put our ideal upon the summit of the mountain, and let it shine out to us as the beacon by which we shall be guided, until we settle it that the only resting point in our search for the truth is the unit, or universal truth, however obtained, until we confirm by repeated examples the verdict of those who have tried to do us justice, we can not emancipate ourselves from our own ignorance and the false notions of the paleface concerning us.

I want to quote a Frenchman who made an unbiased study of American life in 1831. The Gallic mind is always refreshing in its openness. He said: "The Indian in the little they have done have unquestionably displayed as much natural genius as the people of Europe in their most important designs, but nations as well as men require time to learn, whatever may be their intelligence and zeal."

Dr. Franz Boas of Columbia University, the greatest anthropologist in America, claims that so far as his investigations have gone, there is no difference between the brain of a Caucasian and that of an Indian, in actual weight and gray matter.

Besides the research of science, however, we have evidence of the power of abstraction in the Indian mind. History in its true representation gives us credit for generals and statesmen and sages and scholars in such personages as Sitting Bull, Geronimo, Tecumseh, Brant, Sequoia, Logan, and that Indian and statesman once mentioned as a nominee for President of the United States and so many others we have not space for them.[1] The Caucasian discovered these men and since their time, since we have been subjected, there have been others like them, who for want of opportunity have died obscure. . . .

But now what has our red brother actually accomplished with a systematic educational system twenty-five years old? Dismissing the question of his capabilities, what has he actually done, and what has been done for him? What have been his opportunities?

There are altogether 357 government schools; 70 of these reservation boarding schools, 35 non-reservation boarding schools, and 223 day schools. The enrollment in these schools totals 24,500 children. Besides these there are 4,300 children in the mission schools and 11,000 in the public. Of the 11,000, the Five Civilized Tribes of Oklahoma have 6,900.[2] The number of children of the race in school in the country then is 39,800. The last report shows an increase of nearly 2,000 attendance over the year before. Yet there are still 9,000 children without school facilities! . . .

According to the usual method of averages used elsewhere, we should have about 54,000 Indian families. Allowing an average of three children to the family, we would have 162,000 of the young. Discounting the ineligibles, we should have at least 54,000 children of school age. The number accounted for in school and out of school is only 48,000, however, so that we have lost at the lowest estimate 5,200 children somewhere. . . .

. . . Wherever there are boarding schools, and the inmates lead restricted lives and are pinned too closely to the monotony of daily routine, besides being underpaid, we can not expect to find the most progressive there, as a general rule. . . .

---

[1] Kellogg is probably referring to Republican stalwart Charles Curtis, a member of the Kaw tribe of Kansas, who was a congressman (1892–1907) and senator (1907–29) before serving as vice president under Herbert Hoover.

[2] The Cherokees, Choctaws, Creeks, Chickasaws, and Seminoles—all of whom had been removed from the Southeast to Oklahoma in the 1830s—were collectively referred to as the Five Civilized Tribes.

Another objectionable feature of the boarding school is this matter of health. Where there are several hundred together and a large percentage of them are afflicted with trachoma and tuberculosis and the means for their segregation is not sufficient, the well children are open to these dangers. Think of the danger of trachoma. Why, no immigrant can land in New York who has trachoma, but here we are exposing the youth of the race to an incurable disease. If this were done by one individual to another, it would be a penitentiary offense. I hear some one defending the Bureau. Go to the Indian schools and say to the nurses and the doctors that they shall not lose their positions if they will tell you the truth about the health conditions of the schools and we would soon enough find that the hospital equipment in the Indian service is nowhere near adequate to the demand. No one is working at greater disadvantage than this class in the service. . . .

The educative influences are centered in the agency or the schools, and what is the personnel of these institutions? They should be filled with well-paid, efficient social service workers. Instead, they too often need social service themselves. . . .

I would like to be optimistic for the system, but this looks ridiculous to me. . . .

Our future is in the hands of the educational system of today. Those of us who have come thus far know how our youth have longed to reach the summit of the mountain. Let us not forget our own yearnings and the prayers of our ambitious young for opportunity. Let us climb the highest mountain, without looking back till we have reached the top.

Henry Roe Cloud Presents an Alternative Vision of Indian Education

1914

The third document, "Education of the American Indian," is by Henry Roe Cloud (1884–1950), a Winnebago educator who was born near Omaha, Nebraska, on a reservation established for his tribe after it was expelled from Wisconsin in 1837 and subsequently forced to resettle successively in Iowa, Minnesota, and South Dakota. Born Wa-Na-Xi-Lay,

Henry Roe Cloud, "Education of the American Indian," *Quarterly Journal*, 2 (1914): 203–9.

Figure 5.   Henry Roe Cloud.

Studious and devoted to Christianity, Henry Roe Cloud moved from isolated boarding schools to the Mount Hermon Preparatory School in Massachusetts and eventually to Yale University, where he received his bachelor's degree in 1910 and a master's degree in anthropology two years later. Cloud was an active member of the Society of American Indians. The multitalented educator remained active through the 1940s, eventually holding a number of important posts with the Bureau of Indian Affairs. This photograph was taken during the early portion of his career.

The Beinecke Rare Book and Manuscript Library, Yale University.

the young man was renamed Henry Cloud when he enrolled at the government boarding school in Genoa, Nebraska. A brilliant student, Cloud moved on to the Santee Normal Training School, the Northfield Mount Hermon School in Massachusetts, and then Yale College, where he was a member of the class of 1910. Inspired by a missionary couple, Walter and Mary Roe, the young man incorporated their name into his and entered Auburn Theological Seminary. He was ordained a Presbyterian minister in 1913. During his seminary years, Cloud also managed to take graduate courses at Yale and earned a master's degree in the relatively new field of anthropology.

Henry Roe Cloud devoted the bulk of his adult life to the cause of Indian education. In the years immediately following his ordination, he struggled to establish a college preparatory school for Indians. Roe Indian Institute (soon renamed the American Indian Institute) opened in Wichita, Kansas, in 1915. This "Mount Hermon of the West" was the only Indian-run school of its day; it survived until 1930, when financial difficulties caused Roe Cloud to close its doors. From 1931 until his death in 1950, Roe Cloud worked for the Bureau of Indian Affairs, serving as superintendent of the Haskell Indian School in Lawrence, Kansas, and later in various capacities at Indian agencies in Oregon.

The following document is a speech Henry Roe Cloud delivered to the Lake Mohonk Conference, a gathering of Indian reformers and leaders, in the fall of 1914. It reflects the idealism and ambition of a young minister and scholar who was eager to move beyond criticism of the government's educational system and to articulate a vision of Indian schooling that rose above the tired language of "civilization."

The task of educating the American young is a stupendous one. The future welfare of the American nation depends upon it. Children everywhere must be brought into an appreciation of the great fundamental principles of the Republic as well as the full realization of its dangers. . . .

The stupendous economic development has meant the amassing of great and unwieldy wealth into few hands. It has meant the creation of a wide gap between the rich and the poor. . . .

There is the problem of "fire water" that has burned out the souls of hundreds of thousands, to say nothing of the greater suffering of wives, mothers, and children. There is the big national problem of race prejudice. Is America truly to be the "melting pot" of the nations?

These are the problems confronting the white youth, and . . . they are the Indian's problems, also. Besides this, the Indian has his own peculiar race problem to meet.

There is the problem of home education. Education in the home is almost universally lacking. The vast amount of education which the white child receives in the home — a great many of them cultured and Christian homes, where between the age of ten and fourteen the child reads book after book on travel, biography, and current events — goes to make up for the deficiencies of the public schools. The Indian youth goes back into homes that have dominant interests altogether different from what has been taught at school. I have seen many a young man and young woman bravely struggle to change home conditions in order to bring them into keeping with their training, and they have at last gone down. The father and the mother have never been accustomed . . . to a competitive form of existence. The father has no trade or vocation. The value of a dollar, of time, of labor, is unknown in that home. The parents have not the insight into educational values to appreciate the boy's achievements and to inspire him further. What is to be done under such circumstances? In many cases he finds himself face to face with a shattered home. The marriage problem, the very core of his social problem, stares him in the face. Many a young man and woman, realizing these home conditions, have gone away to establish a home of their own. As soon as the thrifty Indian accumulates a little property his relatives and tribesmen, in keeping with the old custom of communal ownership of property, come and live at his expense. There was virtual communal ownership of property in the old days under the unwritten laws of hospitality, but the ommission in these days, of that corresponding equal distribution of labor plays havoc with the young Indian home.

What is the Indian youth to do under such circumstances?

The Indian has his own labor problem. He has here a race inertia to overcome. The sort of labor he is called upon to do these days is devoid of exploit. It is a change from the sporadic effort to that of routine labor calling for the qualities of self-control, patience, steady application, and a long look ahead. Shall he seek labor outside the reservation? Shall he work his own allotment? . . . If he works, how is he to meet the ubiquitous grafter with his insistence upon chattel mortgages? . . .

There is the legal problem. . . . Is the Indian a ward of the government or a citizen? What are his rights and duties? His legal problem involves his land problem. Ought he to pay taxes? Will he ever secure his rights to be respected in the local courts unless he pays taxes? . . .

Shall the Indian youth ignore the problem of religion? Of the many religions on the reservation, which one shall energize his life? Shall it be the sun dance, the medicine lodge, the mescal, or the Christian religion? Shall he take in all religions, as so many do? . . .

There is finally the whole problem of self-support. If he is to pursue the lines of agriculture, he must study the physical environment and topography of his particular reservation, for these in a large measure control the fortunes of his people. . . . The Indian must conquer nature if he is to achieve his race adoption.

My friends, here are problems of unusual difficulty. In the face of these larger problems—city, State, and National, as well as the Indian's own peculiar race problem, and the two are inextricably inter-woven,—what shall be the Indian's preparation to successfully meet them? What sort of education must he have? . . .

The first effort . . . should be to give as many Indians as are able all the education that the problem he faces clearly indicates he should have. This means all the education the grammar schools, secondary schools, and colleges of the land can give him. This is not any too much for the final equipment for the leaders of the race. If we are to have leaders that will supply the disciplined mental power in our race development, they cannot be merely grammar school men. They must be trained to grapple with these economic, educational, political, religious and social problems. They must be men who will take up the righteous cause among their people, interpret civilization to their people, and restore race confidence, race virility. Only by such leaders can race segregation be overcome. Real segregation of the Indian consists in segregation of thought and inequality of education.

We would not be so foolish as to demand a college education for every Indian child in the land irrespective of mental powers and dominant vocational interests, but on the other hand we do not want to make the mistake of advocating a system of education adapted only to the average Indian child. . . . There are hundreds of the youth of . . . other native races in our colleges. As an Indian it is impossible for me to believe that the fact that there are almost no Indians under such training today is due to the failure of my race in mental ability. The difficulty lies in the system rather than in the race. According to the census of the last decade, there were three hundred thousand college men and women to ninety millions of people in the United States, or one to every three hundred. In the same proportion there should be one thousand college Indian men and women in the United States, taking as a total population three hundred thousand Indians. Allowing for racial handicaps, let us say there should be at least five hundred instead of one thousand Indian college men and women. Actually there is not one in thirty thousand, and most of these in early life escaped the retarding process in the Government schools. . . .

. . . I worked two years in turning a washing machine in a Government school to reduce the running expenses of the school. It did not take me long to learn how to run a washing machine. The rest of the two years I nursed a growing hatred for that washing machine. Such work is not educative. It begets a hatred for work, especially where there is no pay for such labor. The Indian will work under such conditions because he is under authority, but the moment he becomes free he is going to get as far as he can from it. . . . The Indian himself must rise up and do for himself by the help of Almighty God. It is to be Christian education, because every problem that confronts us is in the last analysis a moral problem. In the words of Sumner,[1] "Capital is another word for self-denial." The gift of millions for Indian education is the people's self-denial. In whatever activity we may enter for life work, we must pay the price of self-control if we are to achieve any degree of success. The moral qualities, therefore, are so necessary for our successful advance. Where shall we look for our final authority in these moral questions? We must look to nothing this side of the Great Spirit for our final authority. Having then brought into the forefront of the Indian race men of sound morality, intellectual grasp, and productive skill, we shall have leaders who are like the great oak tree on the hill. Storm after storm may break upon them, but they will stand because they are deeply rooted and the texture of their soul is strong.

[1] *William Graham Sumner* (1840–1910), professor of political and social science at Yale University from 1872 to 1909, argued throughout his career that the middle class virtues of thrift and hard work would insure both individual and community advancement. His philosophy came to be called social Darwinism.

Arthur C. Parker Argues
for College Education for Indians
1913

The final document in this chapter is an excerpt from an editorial published in the Society of American Indian's Quarterly Journal *in 1913. Its author, Arthur C. Parker (1881–1955), was a member of a distinguished Seneca family that included Ely Parker, the brigadier general who was the first Native American to serve as commissioner of Indian affairs, and Ely Parker's grandfather, Nicholas H. Parker, who was secretary to the Seneca nation and interpreter for the New York subagency. It is somewhat surprising that this ringing endorsement of advanced learning came from the pen of someone who did not finish college. (Parker attended Dickinson Seminary in Williamsport, Pennsylvania, from 1900 to 1903 but did not graduate.) Less surprising is Parker's declaration that "all civilization does not lie in the ways of the white race," for despite his incomplete education, he had already served for many years as an archaeologist at the New York State Museum. His museum work had brought him into contact with Frederick W. Putnam of Harvard, pioneering ethnologist Frank Speck, and Columbia University's Franz Boas; these patrons in turn introduced him to the emerging field of anthropology. Parker came on the scene just as older notions of "advanced" and "backward" civilizations were being replaced with the idea that all cultures were of equal value. Boas and his students pointed out that every culture sustained practices and cultivated values that served the needs of its members, arguing that no single set of practices and beliefs could be scientifically defended as "superior" to all others. This belief—which came to be called cultural relativism—as well as Parker's support for what today we would call cultural diversity, lies behind the anthropologist's attacks on the government's Indian schools.*

Parker's optimism and idealism were no doubt a reflection of his mixed parentage: His non-Indian mother had been a schoolteacher on the Cattaraugus Reservation, and his father's family moved easily in both white and Indian society in western New York. Parker himself grew up both at Cattaraugus and in White Plains (near New York City) where he attended high school. A passionate defender of Indian interests, the young

Arthur C. Parker, "The Real Value of Higher Education for the Indian," *Quarterly Journal,* 1 (1913): 278–84.

Figure 6.   Arthur C. Parker.
Archaeologist, activist, collector of folklore, and museum administrator, Arthur Parker moved easily between the traditional Seneca communities of upstate New York and the world of white bureaucrats in Washington, D.C., and Rochester, New York. His editorials in the *Quarterly Journal* poked fun at the pretensions of government officials and picked apart the attitude of white supremacy that frequently seeped into official Indian Office pronouncements.
Courtesy of the Edward E. Ayer Collection, The Newberry Library, Chicago.

anthropologist had been one of the founders of the SAI. He was devoted to the organization, serving for five years as editor of its Quarterly Journal, *but he spent most of his career as a museum curator and archeologist. Although Parker was Christian, he was also a devoted student of the teachings of the nineteenth-century Seneca prophet Handsome Lake and published books on many aspects of traditional Iroquois life.*

In the following excerpt Parker replies to the suggestion that a national university be created for American Indians. While acknowledging that it would not be a pancea, Parker embraces the idea of an Indian path to sophisticated learning. The aim was not to imitate whites or fit into their institutions, Parker tells his readers, nor was it to attain a point of "equal ability." Rather, the goal was to strive for "greater ability." Perhaps a new institution could help Indian people attain this goal.

. . . The government Indian school is a very low grade school. It takes Indian pupils to about the eighth grade, a point which white children reach at the age of thirteen or fourteen years. There should be no loud clamor over an Indian reaching this point. Plenty of these Indian boys and girls should then enter high school. *Certainly a "grammar school race" cannot compete with a college bred race.* Why do Americans expect the Indian to succeed in advanced life, when *there is no real preparation* for it?

Scores of Indian high school graduates should enter universities and match brains with the best intellects in the country. Indians should be the peer of the most enlightened. It pays the Indian, and it pays the greater race that holds the country.

In a recent magazine article the editor said that there was a need for an American Indian university. Now remember, *our Society* does *not* say so! No such suggestion is written in its laws or platform. Let no one be frightened if he disagrees, that there is need for an Indian school for higher training. It should not be the high school. Indian students who graduate from government schools should mingle for the four years of high school training with white people in order to accustom themselves to the ways of the country and be freed for a time from their native environment. Then might come the university. "But the ordinary American university! What is the matter, is that not good enough?" See how our critics fly to that question. Yes, we answer, it is good enough for a good many, but still not good enough for the Indian. What the Indian has, ought to be the best. The American university is not the ideal school. It does not produce as high a quality of men as it should. Therefore it is not good enough for the American Indian.

The ideal university would be one which had no prescribed course. It would be one where a man or woman with a fundamental training already acquired might come and develop his mind along the line for which he was best fitted by nature. It would mean a *real unfolding of self and of native genius.* It would be a training that would teach students to think for themselves and to find their own way outward, upward and onward.

The Indian who reached this point would be in no danger of going "back to the blanket." The evil creations of the reservation system would not hurt him. He would clearly see the mission of his race and he would know what great qualities it possessed for development and addition to common culture. Oratory, literature, music, art, architecture, imagination, reverence of nature, love of the Supreme Being— these things the Indian all has within himself. Who is it that scorns these things as pagan, as elements that should make the Indian bend his head in shame! Not I. But do not think as I do—do not believe what I tell you—*consult your own heart.*

There is something greater in life than being like someone else, there is something better in life for the Indian than being like a white man. An imitation is at best a cheap thing and all men of true culture despise it. The Indian must understand the ways of the white race and follow in general the paths of enlightenment, but all civilization does not lie in the ways of the white race—far from it. The white people are sick of themselves and seek comfort and variety in that which is new and refreshing. They are looking for that which rings truer, and breathes of greater purity and simplicity. It is only the ignorant man or the bigot who is satisfied with his own state of culture. The Indian has great things to give the world, but he never can give these things to the world as long as he stays as he is. He must step upward where he can be seen and he must speak where he can be heard. He must use a language and a logic that appeals above the tumult and wins attention. He can do this through education. . . .

3

Discussing Christianity and Religion

From the outset of the European invasion of North America, missionaries and priests labored to convert Native Americans to Christianity. Native leaders in the twentieth century—no less than their counterparts three hundred years earlier—confronted evangelical Christians wherever they encountered advancing settlers or government officials. It was not surprising, therefore, that Indians who criticized "civilization" in the Progressive Era frequently directed some of their comments at Christianity.

Christian ideas and Christian zealots had been fundamental to the European engagement with North America since the age of Columbus. Religious ambition had fueled most of Europe's New World enterprises. It is significant to note, for example, that the first written account of Columbus's 1492 voyage was published in Rome, not in Spain. Ferdinand and Isabella's initial claim to the Western Hemisphere rested on a papal bull granting them the right to evangelize Native peoples. Spain hoped this religious mandate would deter other nations from trying to compete with her New World ambitions. It did not have much effect. In the seventeenth century, France and England sought to outdo Spain in all aspects of overseas expansion. Battalions of French Jesuits were dispatched to the St. Lawrence River valley while the English hoped their Puritan settlers in New England would replace "popish" influences with Protestant ones. While Jamestown's settlers presented their nationalist enterprise as purely commercial, Puritan leader John Winthrop and the Quaker William Penn made religious conversion a central goal of their settlements. (The seal of the Massachusetts Bay Colony featured an Indian figure declaring, "Come over and save me.") Their efforts continued into the eighteenth century. During this period, Spain and France each supported groups of Catholic clerics who spread their influence across the Southwest, to California, and south from Canada into the Mississippi valley. By the time of the American Revolution, these Catholic and Protestant efforts had extended missionary influence to every part of North America except for the Arctic, the western Great Plains, and the Northwest Coast.

After 1776 the architects of U.S. Indian policy followed in the tradition of their colonial forebears. When it came to Indians, they saw no reason to separate religious efforts from political or military concerns. They did not believe the young nation's revolutionary commitment to the separation of church and state should be extended to relations with Native Americans. As a consequence, conversion to Christianity became an important component of federal policy, and federal dollars flowed to religious groups without any public protests. In the nineteenth century the Indian Office regularly supported missionary efforts and religious programs in schools and on reservations. The apex of this cooperative effort came in 1869, when President Grant announced a "peace policy" that involved inviting religious groups to nominate individuals to become Indian agents. Under Grant's program, each major sect was allotted a fixed number of reservations for which they would be responsible. Politics were not forgotten in this process (Grant's own Methodists received a larger share of agencies than the largely Democratic Catholics), but none of its critics raised constitutional objections. In the ensuing decades, the peace policy evolved into assimilationist programs that focused on education and the breakup of reservations into individual land holdings, but religious themes were a continuous thread of federal action. Richard Pratt, for example, the headmaster of the model Carlisle Industrial Training School, raised funds from religious groups to supplement the institution's congressional appropriations. At the same time, church groups dispatched missionaries and educators to reservations to work alongside Indian Office agents. The Presbyterian mission described by Francis La Flesche in chapter 2 is only one example of this phenomenon.

In the first decades of the twentieth century, religious (usually Protestant) rituals were a regular feature of life at government boarding schools, and a number of religious institutions continued to receive federal funds earmarked for "civilization" purposes. Catholics and Protestants battled for influence both in Washington and in tribal communities (and their disputes led to the elimination of direct payments to religious organizations), but both groups continued to believe that any visible evidence of traditional religious traditions (universally condemned as "heathen" practices) was a mark of government failure. Officials also agreed that improving rates of church attendance and evidence of "civilized dress" were measures of government success.

Dissenting views were not welcome. In the 1890s, when anthropologist James Mooney suggested that the recent Ghost Dance movement had emerged from genuine religious longing or when Wild West show promoters expressed admiration for colorful tribal rituals, they were roundly attacked by the Indian Office and the leaders of the major Christian churches. For Progressive Era policymakers both inside and outside the government, the assimilation campaign required Indians to embrace the teaching of Jesus. Criticism of that campaign was understood as an attack on the fundamental tenets of a Christian nation.

In the decades before World War I, Indian Christians themselves began joining the effort to bring the gospel to unconverted Indians. Following in the tradition of Samson Occum, men like the Nez Percé Robert Williams and the Lakota Philip Deloria argued that the Christian faith could guide people through an era of crushing change and dislocation. Progressive Era Christian Indians were more numerous than in earlier eras. Products of mission and government schools, these individuals emerged in every region of the country and were active in nearly every Protestant sect. Indian Catholic priests were rare, but Indian laypeople were active in Catholic community organizations in the Great Lakes, the Great Plains, and the Southwest. At the same time, among the growing number of Native Americans who called themselves Christians were individuals who used their religious beliefs as the basis for criticism of modern American life. In earlier periods, similar critiques had come from Occum; from William Apess, a Pequot who became a Methodist preacher in the 1830s, and from Elias Boudinot, the missionary-trained Cherokee who was the first editor of his tribe's national newspaper.

In the three documents reprinted in this section, Native American leaders express increasingly pointed criticisms of the Christian people and practices they saw around them. The documents reveal the emergence of a biting and wide-ranging critique of contemporary American religious life, and they indicate that Indian criticism of Western religion was growing and becoming more explicit. The first document, "Why I Am a Pagan," is a fictional sketch containing an indirect attack on modern churches; it is not aimed at any individual target. The second, part of a chapter from Charles Eastman's autobiography titled "Civilization as Preached and Practiced," is directed more clearly at contemporary churchgoers, but it is softened somewhat by the fact that it came from an individual who identified himself as a Christian. The third document, statements by Francis La Flesche and Fred Lookout before a congressional committee investigating the rapidly expanding peyote religion, presents the words of individuals who did not bother to describe themselves as Christians and who defended Native practices by declaring that they were profoundly and genuinely religious even though they were not Christian. The trajectory of these statements reflects the growing self-confidence of Native leaders as well as their obvious willingness to expand complaints about religion to broader attacks on American life.

Zitkala Ša (Gertrude Bonnin) Defends Paganism

1902

The daughter of a Yankton woman named Ellen Simmons and a white trader, Gertrude Simmons Bonnin (1876–1938) gave herself the Lakota name Zitkala Ša ("Red Bird") when she began to publish short stories about traditional Sioux life at the turn of the twentieth century. Zitkala Ša had been educated at Quaker schools (White's Indian Manual Labor Institute and Earlham College in Indiana) and had taught at Richard Pratt's industrial training school in Carlisle, Pennsylvania. At Earlham she absorbed a Quaker view of Christianity that rejected formal church rituals and emphasized a personal vision of the Creator. She used her stories to communicate her beliefs to a wider audience as well as to teach about traditional Sioux culture and offer a native perspective on modern life.

The story excerpted below reflects both Zitkala Ša's Quaker education and her growing impatience with Christian missionaries. The narrator makes clear the contrast between the spiritual power of nature and what she sees as the empty piety of many believers—even Indian ones. She is critical of self-important churchgoers—as many Quaker Christians often were—but she praises the beauty and spiritual power of nature. The story first appeared in 1902 and was reprinted in a collection Zitkala Ša called American Indian Stories *in 1921. Her retellings of traditional Sioux tales were collected as* Old Indian Legends *and published in 1901 with illustrations by her Carlisle colleague Angel DeCora, a Winnebago.*

Zitkala Ša, "Why I Am a Pagan," *Atlantic Monthly*, 90 (1902): 801–3.

**Figure 7.
Zitkala Ša.**

Taken in 1921, shortly
after she ended her
term as editor of the
Quarterly Journal, this
portrait of Zitkala Ša
shows her in a tradi-
tional buckskin dress.
Like many activists,
Zitkala Ša had mixed
feelings about appearing
this way: She was eager
to speak about tradi-
tional Sioux culture, but
she did not want her
audiences to forget that
she was an educated
and sophisticated
spokesperson for her
community.
© Bettmann/CORBIS.

Despite her early success as a writer, Zitkala Ša's dissatisfaction with modern American life soon drew her back to her childhood home in South Dakota. In 1902 she left Carlisle and married Raymond T. Bonnin, a Yankton Sioux employee of the Indian Office. Soon Raymond was assigned to the Uintah Ouray Ute Agency in Ft. Duchesne, Utah, and the young couple moved west. Mrs. Bonnin largely gave up writing for the next decade, but she remained interested in Indian affairs and retained her contacts with Richard Pratt, Carlos Montezuma, and other national figures. She joined the Society of American Indians soon after it was

founded in 1911, and in 1916 was offered the position of secretary of the organization, a job that required her to relocate to Washington, D.C.

The Bonnins maintained their Washington home for more than two decades following their move east. Once again appearing as Zitkala Ša, the author edited the Society of American Indians magazine and, following the demise of the SAI in the 1920s, worked with a number of other social welfare organizations, including the General Federation of Women's Clubs and the American Indian Defense Association. In 1926 she and her husband organized the National Congress of American Indians, a group they were able to sustain until her death in 1938. Throughout these years, the Bonnins were tireless advocates of "home rule" for Indians and constant critics of forced assimilation. Zitkala Ša's career stretched nearly forty years beyond the publication of "Why I Am a Pagan," but her actions throughout those years seemed to echo the defiant tone of this early sketch.

When the spirit swells my breast I love to roam leisurely among the green hills; or sometimes, sitting on the brink of the murmuring Missouri, I marvel at the great blue overhead. With half-closed eyes I watch the huge cloud shadows in their noiseless play upon the high bluffs opposite me, while into my ear ripple the sweet, soft cadences of the river's song. Folded hands lie in my lap, for the time forgot. My heart and I lie small upon the earth like a grain of throbbing sand. Drifting clouds and tinkling waters, together with the warmth of a genial summer day, bespeak with eloquence the loving Mystery round about us. During the idle while I sat upon the sunny river brink, I grew somewhat, though my response be not so clearly manifest as in the green grass fringing the edge of the high bluff back of me.

At length retracing the uncertain footpath scaling the precipitous embankment, I seek the level lands where grow the wild prairie flowers. And they, the lovely little folk, soothe my soul with their perfumed breath. . . .

With these thoughts I reach the log cabin whither I am strongly drawn by the tie of a child to an aged mother. Out bounds my four-footed friend to meet me, frisking about my path with unmistakable delight. Chän is a black shaggy dog, "a thorough bred little mongrel" of whom I am very fond. Chän seems to understand many words in Sioux, and will go to her mat even when I whisper the word, though generally I think she is guided by the tone of the voice. Often she tries

to imitate the sliding inflection and long drawn out voice to the amusement of our guests, but her articulation is quite beyond my ear. In
both my hands I hold her shaggy head and gaze into her large brown
eyes. At once the dilated pupils contract into tiny black dots, as if the
roguish spirit within would evade my questioning.

Finally resuming the chair at my desk I feel a keen sympathy with
my fellow creatures, for I seem to see clearly again that all are akin.

The racial lines, which once were bitterly real, now serve nothing
more than marking out a living mosaic of human beings. And even
here men of the same color are like the ivory keys of one instrument
where each resembles all the rest, yet varies from them in pitch and
quality of voice. And those creatures who are for a time mere echoes
of another's note are not unlike the fable of the thin sick man whose
distorted shadow, dressed like a real creature, came to the old master
to make him follow as a shadow. Thus with a compassion for all echoes
in human guise, I greet the solemn-faced "native preacher" whom I
find awaiting me. I listen with respect for God's creature, though he
mouthed most strangely the jangling phrases of a bigoted creed.

And as our tribe is one large family, where every person is related
to all the others, he addresses me:

"Cousin, I came from the morning church service to talk with you."

"Yes?" I said interrogatively, as he paused for some word from me.

Shifting uneasily about in the straight-backed chair he sat upon, he
began: "Every holy day [Sunday] I look about our little God's house,
and not seeing you there, I am disappointed. This is why I come today.
Cousin, as I watch you from afar, I see no unbecoming behavior and
hear only good reports of you, which all the more burns me with the
wish that you were a church member. Cousin, I was taught long years
ago by kind missionaries to read the holy book. These godly men
taught me also the folly of our old beliefs.

"There is one God who gives reward or punishment to the race of
dead men. In the upper region the Christian dead are gathered in
unceasing song and prayer. In the deep pit below, the sinful ones
dance in torturing flames.

"Think upon these things, my cousin, and choose now to avoid the
after-doom of hell fire!" Then followed a long silence in which he
clasped tighter and unclasped again his interlocking fingers.

Like instantaneous lightning flashes came pictures of my own
mother's making, for she, too, is now a follower of the new superstition.

"Knocking out the chinking of our log cabin, some evil hand thrust
in a burning taper of braided dry grass, but failed of his intent, for the

fire died out and the half-burned brand fell inward to the floor. Directly above it, on a shelf, lay the holy book. This is what we found after our return from a several days' visit. Surely some great power is hid in the sacred book!"

Brushing away from my eyes many like pictures, I offered midday meal to the converted Indian sitting wordless and with downcast face. No sooner had he risen from the table with "Cousin, I have relished it," than the church bell rang.

Thither he hurried forth with his afternoon sermon. I watched him as he hastened along, his eyes bent fast upon the dusty road till he disappeared at the end of a quarter of a mile.

The little incident recalled to mind the copy of a missionary paper brought to my notice a few days ago, in which a "Christian" pugilist commented upon a recent article of mine, grossly perverting the spirit of my pen. Still I would not forget that the pale-faced missionary and the hoodooed aborigine are both God's creatures, though small indeed their own conceptions of Infinite Love. A weak child toddling in a wonder world, I prefer to their dogma my excursions into the natural gardens where the voice of the Great Spirit is heard in the twittering of birds, the rippling of mighty waters, and the sweet breathing of flowers. If this is Paganism, then, at present, at least, I am a Pagan.

Charles Eastman Compares the Morality of Indians and Modern Christians

1916

Probably the best-known Indian of his generation, Charles Eastman (1858–1939) struck most whites as the epitome of civilization. Brought to the Presbyterian Santee Training School in Flandreau, South Dakota, at the age of fourteen, the young man had exchanged his tribal name, Ohiyesa ("the Winner") for Eastman and had blazed a path of distinction through several institutions, including Dartmouth College (class of 1887) and Boston University Medical School (M.D., 1890). He served as an agency physician at Pine Ridge, South Dakota, until 1893, when,

Charles Eastman, "Civilization as Preached and Practiced" in *From the Deep Woods to Civilization* (Boston: Little, Brown, 1916), 136–50, 193–95.

Figure 8.   Charles Eastman.
The most prominent American Indian leader of his generation, Eastman had experience as a government official,
YMCA organizer, author, lecturer, and political lobbyist. His
books brought traditional Native American culture before a
broad non-Indian audience and played a crucial role in culti-
vating a sympathetic audience for Native concerns.
Courtesy of the Edward E. Ayer Collection, The Newberry Library,
Chicago.

*disgusted with the government's insensitive bureaucracy, he resigned to
establish a private medical practice in St. Paul, Minnesota.*

*The following excerpt from Eastman's autobiography describes his
decision in the late 1890s to become a field organizer for the YMCA. At
that point in his career his practice was only marginally successful and*

he was deeply worried about supporting his young wife (Elaine Goodale, a school teacher from Massachusetts whom he had met at Pine Ridge) and growing family. He worked for the YMCA only until 1898, but his duties setting up new reservation chapters of the organization gave him the opportunity to travel and speak with Indians in several parts of the country. As he indicates in the passage reprinted below, Eastman's experience clarified some of the differences between modern American culture and the values embedded in traditional Indian cultures. As is also clear, the experience provided interesting material for speeches and essays.

Eastman began writing sketches of Indian life and descriptions of his own boyhood at the urging of his wife. He first published stories in children's magazines, but interest was great enough to generate invitations to write for a general audience. A memoir, Indian Boyhood *(1902), was his first book. It was followed by several collections of stories, reflections on Indian culture such as* The Soul of the Indian *(1911), and a full-length autobiography,* From The Deep Woods to Civilization, *published in 1916.*

Eastman's work with the YMCA also marked the waning of his career as a private physician. Tired of struggling to win the confidence of white patients, he found writing and involvement in Indian affairs far more rewarding. He tried the Indian Office again from 1900 to 1903, but he left his post as agency physician to serve in other capacities for the government, to lecture, and to travel. He and his wife finally settled in Amherst, Massachusetts, not far from her childhood home. Eastman was one of the founders of the Society of American Indians and was active in that organization until it collapsed in the 1920s. In his later years Eastman grew increasingly disillusioned with modern life. He separated from his wife and spent much of his time alone in a cabin in the Canadian woods in southern Ontario.

The following excerpt reflects Eastman at his most outspoken. It was written at a moment when the Society of American Indians was gaining influence. Eastman was at the height of his career as an activist and public lecturer. While clearly committed to life in white society, he struggled here to bridge the distance between his "civilized" identity and his warmly remembered childhood. How ironic, his readers must have thought, that a man so deeply invested in the American present was also so deeply attached to his tribal past.

... One day a stranger called on me in my office. He was, I learned, one of the field secretaries of the International Committee of Y.M.C.A. and had apparently called to discuss the feasibility of extending this movement among the Indians. After we had talked for some time, he broached the plan of putting a man into the Indian field, and ended by urging me to consider taking up the work. . . . I doubted my fitness for religious work. He still pressed me to accept, pointing out the far-reaching importance of this new step, and declared that they had not been able to hear of any one else of my race so well fitted to undertake it. We took the matter under consideration, and with some reluctance I agreed to organize the field. . . .

. . . I traveled over a large part of the western states and in Canada, visiting the mission stations among Indians of all tribes, and organizing young men's associations wherever conditions permitted. I think I organized some forty-three associations. This gave me a fine opportunity to study Protestant missionary effort among Indians. I seriously considered the racial attitude toward God, and almost unconsciously reopened the book of my early religious training, asking myself how it was that our simple lives were so imbued with the spirit of worship, while much church-going among white and nominally Christian Indians led often to such very small results.

A new point of view came to me then and there. This latter was a machine-made religion. It was supported by money, and more money could only be asked for on the showing made; therefore too many of the workers were after quantity rather than quality of religious experience.

I was constantly meeting with groups of young men of the Sioux, Cheyennes, Crees, Ojibways, and others, in log cabins or little frame chapels, and trying to set before them in simple language the life and character of the Man Jesus. I was cordially received everywhere, and always listened to with the closest attention. Curiously enough, even among these men who were seeking light on the white man's ideals, the racial philosophy emerged from time to time.

I remember one old battle-scarred warrior who sat among the young men got up and said, in substance: "Why, we have followed this law you speak of for untold ages! We owned nothing, because everything is from Him. Food was free, land free as sunshine and rain. Who has changed all this? The white man; and yet he says he is a believer in God! He does not seem to inherit any of the traits of his Father, nor does he follow the example set by his brother Christ."

Another of the older men had attentively followed our Bible study and attended every meeting for a whole week. I finally called upon him for his views. After a long silence he said:

"I have come to the conclusion that this Jesus was an Indian. He was opposed to material acquirement and to great possessions. He was inclined to peace. He was as unpractical as any Indian and set no price upon his labor of love. These are not the principles upon which the white man has founded his civilization. It is strange that he could not rise to these simple principles which were commonly observed among our people."

These words put the spell of an uncomfortable silence upon our company, but it did not appear that the old man had intended any sarcasm or unkindness, for after a minute he added that he was glad we had selected such an unusual character for our model. . . .

Among other duties of my position, I was expected to make occasional speaking trips through the East to arouse interest in the work, and it thus happened that I addressed large audiences in Chicago, New York, Boston, and at Lake Mohonk.[1] I was taken by slum and settlement workers to visit the slums and dives of the cities, which gave another shock to my ideals of "Christian civilization." Of course, I had seen something of the poor parts of Boston during my medical course, but not at night, and not in a way to realize the horror and wretchedness of it as I did now. To be sure, I had been taught even as a child that there are always some evil-minded men in every nation, and we knew well what it is to endure physical hardship, but our poor lost nothing of their self-respect and dignity. Our great men not only divided their last kettle of food with a neighbor, but if great grief should come to them, such as the death of a child or wife, they would voluntarily give away their few possessions and begin life over again in token of their sorrow. We could not conceive of the extremes of luxury and misery existing thus side by side, for it was common observation with us that the coarse weeds, if permitted to grow, will choke out the more delicate flowers. These things troubled me very much; yet I still held before my race the highest, and as yet unattained, ideals of the white man.

One of the strongest rebukes I ever received from an Indian for my acceptance of these ideals and philosophy was administered by an old chief of the Sac and Fox tribe in Iowa.[2] I was invited to visit them by the churches of Toledo and Tama City, which were much concerned by the absolute refusal of this small tribe to accept civilization and Christianity. I surmise that these good people hoped to use me as an example of the benefits of education for the Indian.

[1]Beginning in 1883, a group of religious leaders and advocates of reform would gather each fall at the Lake Mohonk Lodge, a resort owned by a Quaker family, to discuss Indian issues.

[2]The modern Mesquakie community in Tama, Iowa.

I was kindly received at their village, and made, as I thought, a pretty good speech, emphasizing the necessity of educating their children, and urging their acceptance of the Christian religion. The old chief rose to answer. He was glad that I had come to visit them. He was also glad that I was apparently satisfied with the white man's religion and his civilization. As for them, he said, neither of these had seemed good to them. The white man had showed neither respect for nature nor reverence toward God, but, he thought, tried to buy God with the by-products of nature. He tried to buy his way into heaven, but he did not even know where heaven is.

"As for us," he concluded, "we shall still follow the old trail. If you should live long, and some day the Great Spirit shall permit you to visit us again, you will find us still Indians, eating with wooden spoons out of bowls of wood. I have done."

I was even more impressed a few minutes later, when one of his people handed me my pocket book containing my railway tickets and a considerable sum of money. I had not even missed it! I said to the state missionary who was at my side, "Better let these Indians alone! If I had lost my money in the streets of your Christian city, I should probably have never seen it again."

My effort was to make the Indian feel that Christianity was not at fault for the white man's sins, but rather the lack of it, and I freely admitted that this nation is not Christian, but declared that the Christians in it are trying to make it so. I found the facts and the logic of them often hard to dispute, but was partly consoled by the wonderful opportunity to come into close contact with the racial mind, and to refresh my understanding of the philosophy in which I had been trained, but which had been overlaid and superseded by a college education. I do not know how much good I accomplished, but I did my best.

[Eastman concluded his autobiography with a chapter titled "The Soul of the White Man," in which he reflected on his relationship with Christian civilization.]

... From the time I first accepted the Christ ideal it has grown upon me steadily, but I also see more and more plainly our modern divergence from that ideal. I confess I have wondered much that Christianity is not practised by the very people who vouch for that wonderful conception of exemplary living. It appears that they are anxious to pass on their religion to all races of men, but keep very little of it themselves. I have not yet seen the meek inherit the earth, or the peacemakers receive high honor.

Why do we find so much evil and wickedness practised by the nations composed of professedly "Christian" individuals? The pages of history are full of licensed murder and the plundering of weaker and less developed peoples, and obviously the world to-day has not out-grown this system. Behind the material and intellectual splendor of our civilization, primitive savagery and cruelty and lust hold sway, undiminished, and as it seems, unheeded. When I let go of my simple, instinctive nature religion, I hoped to gain something far loftier as well as more satisfying to the reason. Alas! It is also more confusing and contradictory. The higher and spiritual life, though first in theory, is clearly secondary, if not entirely neglected, in actual practice. When I reduce civilization to its lowest terms, it becomes a system of life based upon trade. The dollar is the measure of value, and *might* still spells *right;* otherwise, why war?

Yet even in deep jungles God's own sunlight penetrates, and I stand before my own people still as an advocate of civilization. Why? First, because there is no chance for our former simple life any more; and second, because I realize that the white man's religion is not respon-sible for his mistakes. There is every evidence that God has given him all the light necessary by which to live in peace and good-will with his brother; and we also know that many brilliant civilizations have col-lapsed in physical and moral decadence. It is for us to avoid their fate if we can.

Francis La Flesche and Fred Lookout Defend Peyote before Congress

1918

In 1918 congressional hearings on legislation to outlaw the use of the peyote cactus (Lophophera williamsii) in religious rituals brought to the surface sharply differing views of traditional Indian culture. For cen-turies, Peyote had been used by Rio Grande peoples in religious ceremo-nies that practitioners believed helped them communicate with the Creator. These practitioners would ingest "buttons" of peyote or sip tea brewed from the plant during an extended period of praying and drumming. The

Hearings Before a Subcommittee of the Committee on Indian Affairs on H.R. 2614, 1918, House Committee on Indian Affairs, 114, 149–55.

all-night ritual frequently produced visions that instructed individuals on how to live their lives. Many tribal religious leaders resisted the use of peyote because it undermined their own community's traditional practices. However, in the early twentieth century, a combination of economic despair in many southwestern communities, the decline of tribal rituals, and efficient rail links that allowed practitioners to ship peyote to fellow believers hundreds of miles away helped extend a new version of the ritual across the West. Tribal communities in Oklahoma were the first to begin importing and using peyote from Texas. Soon religious leaders— called "roadmen"—began spreading the practice to the Plains and Canada and west to New Mexico and Arizona. This new faith coupled group meetings promising visionary experiences with the basic elements of Christianity and a strict insistence that believers practice monogamy, work, and swear off alcohol. After attending peyote meetings, many practitioners declared that they had spoken with the Creator (or Jesus) and had been persuaded to take up a new life.

Office of Indian Affairs agents and missionaries tried to suppress the new "peyote religion," but the absence or inconsistency of state prohibition laws hampered their efforts. The Indian Office then turned to Congress to pass a general law banning the use or transportation of the cactus. Practitioners responded by organizing themselves into a religious sect, the Native American Church, and claimed that the government's efforts violated the First Amendment to the U.S. Constitution.

A number of Native American leaders—including Zitkala Ša and Charles Eastman—opposed the use of peyote, but speaking in defense of the new ritual were other Native leaders such as Francis La Flesche, anthropologists, and members of the Native American Church who believed the new faith provided a positive avenue for poverty-stricken reservation residents. Among the most eloquent of peyote's defenders were La Flesche, then working for the Smithsonian Institution, and Fred Lookout. La Flesche had grown more outspoken in his criticism of the government since the publication of The Middle Five *eighteen years earlier. He had witnessed the advent of the peyote rite among his own tribe, the Omaha, and had spoken with a number of the religion's adherents in Oklahoma. While he made it clear he was not a practitioner, La Flesche spoke as an anthropologist who respected all sincere expressions of religious faith and who had not been able to detect any harmful side effects among those who regularly used peyote in their gatherings.*

La Flesche's companion before the Congressional committee, Fred Lookout (1865–1949), was an Oklahoma Osage leader who spoke about the new faith from personal experience. Lookout had been born in

Figure 9. Fred Lookout.
A graduate of Captain Pratt's Carlisle Industrial Training School, Lookout was a longtime member of the Osage Tribal Council. He served as principal chief of the tribe for a total of twenty-six years between 1914 and 1949. Throughout this period Lookout was a steadfast advocate of the use of peyote in religious rituals and a national leader in the new Native American Church.
Museum of American History, Smithsonian Institution.

*Kansas before his tribe had been forced out of that state and confined to
an Oklahoma reservation. The son of a tribal leader, he had been singled
out for education and sent to the Carlisle school soon after it opened in
1879. He returned to Oklahoma in 1884. Lookout began to farm an
allotment on the Osage Reservation and, thanks to his education and
family connections, he soon emerged as a tribal leader. He became a
member of the Osage Tribal Council in 1908 and served on that body for
most of the next forty years. He held the elected position of principal chief
for twenty-six years. His political career involved him in the management
of the Osage oil leases and made him a witness to the tragic divisions
among the Osage that attended the great wealth accompanying the oil
boom. Throughout his career Lookout maintained a reputation for hon-
esty and competence. He sought to balance traditional loyalties against
the demands of business and the forces of modernization, maintaining
that the Native American Church provided the moral and religious
framework for navigating a way through these competing interests. As he
told the committee in 1918, with peyote the Osages had lived "a whole lot
better life."*

*The following excerpt is taken from hearings held in connection with
one proposal to ban peyote.*

Statement of Mr. Francis La Flesche,
Bureau of American Ethnology, an Omaha Indian

Mr. Francis La Flesche: I have had numerous opportunities to study
the use of the peyote among the Poncas, the Osage, and my own
people, the Omahas. I had heard extraordinary stories told about
its effects, about the immorality that it produced, and about the
promiscuity of the people who used the peyote at their meetings. I
expected to find evidence of the truth of these stories.

When I went among the Osage people, some of the leaders of
the peyote religion were anxious for me to attend their meetings,
and wishing to know what effect this "medicine," as they called it,
had upon each individual, I accepted the invitation. I attended a
meeting at which . . . Mr. Arthur Bonnicastle [who had testified earlier the same day] was present, and sat with him. At about 6 o'clock
in the evening the people entered their "meeting house" and sat in
a circle around a fire kindled over some symbolic figures marked in
the center of a shallow excavation in the middle of the room. The
peyote was passed around, some of it in pellets of the consistency

of dough, and some prepared in liquid form. The drum was cere-monially circulated and accompanied by singing. From all that I had heard of the intoxicating effects of the peyote I expected to see the people get gloriously drunk and behave as drunken people do. While I sat waiting to see fighting and some excitement the singing went on and on and I noticed that all gazed at the fire or beyond, at a little mound on top of which lay a single peyote. I said to the man sitting next to me, "What do you expect to see?" He said, "We expect to see the face of Jesus and the face of our dead relatives. We are worshiping God and Jesus, the same God that the white people worship." All night long the singing went on and I sat watch-ing the worshipers. It was about 5 o'clock in the morning when sud-denly the singing ceased, the drum and the ceremonial staff were put away, and the leader, beginning at the right of the door, asked each person: "What did you see?" Some replied, "I saw nothing." Others said, "I saw the face of Jesus and it made me happy." Some answered, "I saw the faces of my relatives, and they made me glad." And so on, around the entire circle. I noticed that there were only a few who had been able to see faces, the greater number of the men and women saw nothing. It was explained to me by the leader that these revelations come quickly to those whose thoughts and deeds are pure. To those who are irreverent, they come slowly, although they may come in time. This meeting, as well as others that I have been permitted to attend, was as orderly as any religious meeting I have seen in this and other cities.

I am thoroughly convinced that these Indians are worshiping God in their own simple way, and if their religion is interfered with by the Government or anybody else, and it is suppressed, the con-sequences will be very grave. . . .

The persons who are opposed to the use of the peyote by the Indians in their religion say that it makes them immoral. That has not been my observation. The Indians who have taken the new reli-gion strive to live upright moral lives, and I think their morality can be favorably compared with that of any community of a like number in this country. . . .

This is a matter of religion that the Indian Office and the mis-sionaries are attacking. The Omaha members of this new religion, and of whom I now speak, strive to refrain from the use of whisky. Some of them—a very few indeed—fail to live up to the teachings against drunkenness and use both peyote and whisky, but as a rule the members refrain from the use of whisky, lemon extracts, and wines. I know this because I have frequently visited them in their homes.

Some persons who are opposed to the peyote say that the Indian will pray only when he is under the influence of the peyote. This is not true of my Omaha friends. I was at my brother's house one day, and the sun was just setting on a summer's day, and his wife said, "We will set the table outside; the house is warm. So the table was set outside and we gathered around it. My brother is not a peyote man, but as a prominent member of the new religion happened to be present as a guest, my brother set before this man a glass of water and said to him, "Will you ask the blessing for us?" The man had not taken any peyote, but without any hesitation he put his hand over the water and asked God to bless it. The members of this new religion use the water as a symbol of purity. When the man had asked for the blessing, the water was passed around, and each person present took a sip of it. The man said, "Oh, God, bless this water and let it cleanse our spirits, let it cleanse our minds so that we can understand You." That was the burden of his prayer. And he also asked that his people might be kept from drunkenness, that their souls might be kept pure. That is what he prayed for. He prayed intelligently.

The new religion of which the peyote is a part has been the means of delivering the Omahas from a desperate situation of drunkenness, and so I, for one, will say, "Let the peyote stay among the Indians." It is a part of their religion; it is something that they depend upon for their morality; it is an aid to them. They do not worship it, but they worship God. . . .

Somebody has very unkindly said that these peyote people are lazy and will not work. I do not think this to be true. About two years ago I was on the Omaha Reservation. A fair was being held there under the supervision of the representative of the Indian Office. The Omaha people were bringing their cattle, their hogs, their turkeys, chickens, and other farm products for exhibition. The people camped in a wide circle as they displayed their products, and many of those who drew prizes were peyote people.

Statement of Fred Lookout, Chief
of the Osage Tribe of Indians, Pawhuska, Okla.

Mr. Fred Lookout: We use this peyote in the worship of God among the Osage Indians. We worship it in a manner that is the right way. We are praying to God when we use this medicine that is known as peyote, and the Osage people, my people, use it to a certain extent. They use it in the right way. There is no harm in it. I like it and I am in favor of it. . . .

. . . When I use it I use it in the right way. . . . The Osage people, as a member of the tribe, I know use it in the right way, and we use it like people going to church. We have our regular meetings. We do not use this peyote every day. We do not use it everywhere we go. We use it in the right way. We have church houses, ourselves, among the Osage people. We have our gatherings there and worship to God and use this peyote as we think is the better way amongst our own people. I use it myself and I know by using it I live in a better way, and I like it on that account. My people are doing very well, and for that reason I like the use of this peyote. Since the use of peyote amongst the Osage Indians my young people, or my young men, have developed quite a good reputation. They are living up to their words. They are living under the laws of the State where we live. They are prosperous; they are gaining; and they are living a better life and making money, settling down in their own homesteads and raising their own cattle and horses and everything. By using this peyote they have lived a whole lot better life. On the other hand, before they began to use peyote, my people would use whisky and it ruined a lot of our people. They would ruin their lives and ruin their homes. They did not have anything. They have gone to nothing, and since the use of this peyote they have gained. I recognized the way they were doing and this is the reason I am in favor of this peyote. I want the committee to hear what I have got to say. And that is all.

Mr. Tillman:[1] What effect has peyote upon you when you use it?

Chief Lookout: It does not have any effect upon me. When I eat this peyote I worship with it; that is, I worship God Almighty. It does not have any effect on me. . . .

Mr. Tillman: How many members of your tribe use peyote?

Chief Lookout: Most all the full-blood members of the tribe.

Mr. Tillman: Is this a Christian religion, or is it a mere worship of peyote, or the drug itself?

Chief Lookout: We worship God Almighty; we worship to Him.

Mr. Tillman: Then explain to this committee where you get any authority from the Bible for the use of this bean in worship?

[1]*Benjamin Tillman:* a Democratic congressman from South Carolina.

Chief Lookout: I do not understand about the Bible. If the Bible gives any authority for the use of this peyote, I am not familiar with it.

Mr. Tillman: Then where do you get your authority for the use of it?

Chief Lookout: All of my people use this peyote, and some other members of the tribe came to me and persuaded me to use it. That is how I came to use it. . . .

. . . I am a member of the peyote; I eat this peyote; I do not get lazy; I am on a farm; several of the men have visited my farm; the Commissioner of Indian Affairs has been to my home; I am farming there, and have several stock, and I am doing what I can to make money; I do not get lazy; I do not think the other Indians get lazy either, among the members. . . .

Mr. Snyder:[2] What do you say as to the stability and the physical ability of these people today as compared to 11 years ago when you started to use peyote?

Chief Lookout: They are better; they are better people now; they feel better.

Mr. Snyder: Do they work better?

Chief Lookout: Yes, sir; they work better.

Mr. Snyder: Do you believe that the farms and the industries of that section of the country are in a better productive condition today than they were 11 years ago when you commenced to use peyote?

Chief Lookout: They are.

Mr. Snyder: What would these 400 full-blood Indians do for a religion if peyote were taken away from them?

Chief Lookout: It would ruin the Osage to stop the use of this peyote. They will go back to the back-life; they will go to drinking whisky or do anything. They will not try to gain anything if this peyote stops; it will be a ruin to my tribe, and that is the reason I am talking in favor of it.

[2]*Homer Snyder:* a Republican congressman from New York.

4

American Indians
on America's Indian Policy

During the Progressive Era, the educated Indian leaders who joined the Society of American Indians or spoke out in the political arena were sympathetic to the fundamental goals of U.S. Indian policy. Anchored by the General Allotment Act, which mandated the gradual transformation of communally owned reservations into communities of independent farmers living on individually owned tracts of land, national policy promised to "assimilate" Native people into the general American population. In addition to promoting individual land ownership, federal programs promised to provide literacy, gradual citizenship, and rudimentary "job training" to individuals wishing to be farmers or unskilled workers. Many Native leaders who spoke out in the early twentieth century generally embraced this offer.

Government programs in place in the first decade of the twentieth century had largely been conceived in the 1870s and 1880s, a period when the idealism of the Civil War era was slipping into memory and the closely balanced power of Republicans and Democrats limited political leadership. In this atmosphere, "Indian reform" struck a resonant note, particularly with congressional Republicans. Promising "justice" to Native Americans was politically easy—land and education for Indians generated none of the backlash produced by similar proposals for African Americans. The promise of "equality" for Indians threatened few white voters, particularly when the bulk of the tribes lived in federal territories and sent no voting delegates to Congress. Policymakers launched the assimilationist agenda with nearly unanimous congressional support. It should not be surprising, then, that at the turn of the twentieth century graduates of federal Indian boarding schools and Christian Indian leaders saw no alternative to the government's programs.

But as the new century got underway, it was becoming evident that the terms of the government's bright promises of a generation earlier were being unilaterally changed. The allotment of reservation lands to individual tribal members, conceived in the 1880s as a gradual process that would unfold over several decades, suddenly appeared to be taking place all at once. Ten western states joined the Union between 1889 and 1912, dramatically increasing the region's representation in Congress. Pressure increased for rapid allotment. White westerners saw quickly that dividing large reservations into 160-acre parcels would use only a small portion of the total tribal land base. Consequently they were eager to accelerate the allotment process so that individual tribal members received their homesteads. Their efforts received a significant boost in 1903 when the Supreme Court ruled in *Lone Wolf v. Hitchcock* that the Indian Office was no longer required to follow treaty procedures when negotiating for the sale of these "surplus" tribal lands. It could therefore allot the reservations and seize surplus tribal lands without the consent of the tribes involved.[1]

After the *Lone Wolf* decision, Congress was free to approve statutes that divided a reservation into allotments and classified the remaining tribal estate as "public land," open to homesteaders and cattlemen. The Indian Office praised this new approach. In his 1903 report, for example, Commissioner of Indian Affairs William Jones declared, "The pressure for land must diminish the reservations . . . so that the balance may become homes for white farmers who require them."[2] In the decade before World War I, allotment came to dozens of large reservations where tribal lands were opened to homesteading and the objections of tribal leaders were routinely ignored.

The increasingly authoritarian tone of Indian policymaking was also reflected in education programs and the administration of tribal agencies. The notion that Natives had been supported long enough and should now find their own way in the world became popular in Congress and in the Indian Office bureaucracy. Schools, for example, emphasized vocational training rather than an education aimed at preparing children for citizenship. Vocational lessons often included "instruction" in "cooking" and "farming," which in practice meant that

[1]The *Lone Wolf* case involved the Kiowa Reservation in Oklahoma. Congress had provided for the disposal of surplus lands without securing the approval of the tribe as required by treaty. In its decision the justices declared that Congress had "plenary authority" in Indian affairs and therefore was free to act in any way it chose.

[2]*Annual Report of the Commissioner of Indian Affairs,* U.S. Commission of Indian Affairs. *Annual Report* (Washington, D.C.: Government Printing Office, 1903), 3.

children were put to work in the kitchens and gardens of the schools in order to reduce operating costs. Agents shifted children to the local public schools in an effort to lower enrollments (and expenses) at agency schools. While explained as promoting the "assimilation" of Indians, this shift to public schools usually occurred without federal oversight; thus, no steps were taken to overcome local anti-Indian prejudices or supervise attendance. Freed from the agency schools and unwelcome in classrooms supported by local white taxpayers, Indian children exhibited little enthusiasm for the new arrangement. Finally, agents proudly announced that declining numbers of their charges relied on government rations for survival. God's injunction to Adam that he was fated to earn his living "by the sweat of his brow" became a staple refrain in Congress and the Indian Office.

Many of the young Native American leaders who spoke out in the early twentieth century found themselves caught between the demands being imposed on modern Indian communities—to become self-sufficient and to conform to white expectations—and the benevolent promises that had been made to them in their youth. In the nineteenth century they had been promised membership in a compassionate and charitable nation; in the twentieth century their brethren were being ordered to jump quickly on board an accelerating industrial juggernaut. It seemed clear that the "equality" promised a generation earlier had been redefined in the coldly competitive atmosphere of the twentieth century. They were now free to survive on their own. If they could not escape poverty and powerlessness, it was probably their own fault. Talking back to this new industrial view of the world, Progressive Era Indian leaders often emphasized the government's failure to protect their communities from greedy settlers, as well as its tendency to fall back on authoritarian tactics when enforcing Indian Office policy. Critics of federal policy called for either a renewal of the commitment to help Indian people or (believing that an era of federal benevolence was unlikely ever to occur) the elimination of federal controls over their communities. Instead of proposing a new set of laws or policies, many Indian Progressives favored freedom from the power and control of the Indian Office.

It is important to recall the context in which the following statements were composed because on first inspection they may strike modern readers as timid or contradictory. The authors of these statements make explicit their loyalty to the United States and their endorsement of assimilation. At the same time, however, they insist that federal officials recognize Indian people as a distinctive group within

American society and that past agreements, whether implicit in government policy or formally incorporated into treaties, be honored. Beneath the loyal rhetoric a careful reader can detect both rage over the government's cavalier and patronizing actions, and a determination that Indian people be seen as fellow human beings and fellow citizens. Like other Progressive reformers of their day, these Indian leaders sought government action that would be both efficient and compassionate. They called not for a new bureaucracy but for a new relationship between American Indians and the American government.

Carlos Montezuma Advocates the Abolition of the Indian Office
1914

Carlos Montezuma (1866?–1923) was easily the most outspoken Indian critic of government policy during the Progressive Era. While he joined with other educated Native Americans in founding the Society of American Indians and calling for greater public understanding of Indian history and culture, he argued more forcefully than anyone else that the Indian Office, the bureaucracy responsible for Indian "uplift," should be abolished. His stand was no doubt related to his personal history, for Montezuma was a self-made man.

Named Wassaja by his Yavapai parents, Montezuma was born into the turmoil of territorial Arizona. In 1871, amid a swirl of gold prospectors, white settlers, and intertribal raiders, he was taken prisoner by a group of Pima men and sold to an itinerant photographer for thirty dollars. The photographer, Carlos Gentile, renamed the boy after himself, adding the name of the Aztec king as a stylish flourish. Gentile took Carlos Montezuma with him when he returned to the Midwest, eventually placing him in the care of a Baptist minister in Urbana, Illinois. A star student, Montezuma excelled in his classes, graduating from the University of Illinois with a degree in chemistry and then, in 1889, from Chicago Medical College, where he earned his medical degree. Montezuma served as a reservation physician and as a medical officer at the Carlisle school in the 1890s, but by the end of the decade he had moved

Carlos Montezuma, "What Indians Must Do," *Quarterly Journal,* 2 (1914): 294–9.

Figure 10.   Carlos Montezuma.
At the age of six, Carlos Montezuma was captured from his
Yavapai family by Pima Indians near Florence, Arizona.
Before long, an itinerant photographer, Carlos Gentile,
bought the boy from his captors and renamed the youth after
himself and the Aztec emperor. By the time he sat for this
portrait, Montezuma had graduated from the University of
Illinois and Chicago Medical College and had established a
successful medical practice. Montezuma's remarkable success fueled his determination to end all government regulation of Indian life.
National Anthropological Archives, Smithsonian Institution.

back to Chicago and established a private practice. Although he main-
tained his ties to Carlisle's founder, Richard Henry Pratt, Montezuma
also began to seek out his relatives in Arizona. These contacts and his
continuing relationship with Pratt gradually drew him into Indian
affairs.

Proud of his own achievements, Montezuma was appalled at the incompetence and paternalism of the Indian Office. He gradually came to the conclusion that no progress was possible for Indians unless the agency went out of business. He helped found the Society of American Indians in 1911 but quickly determined that the group was not committed enough to the abolition of the Indian Office. In response he created his own newsletter, Wassaja, *in 1916, in which he spoke out forcefully on the evils of the Indian Office. As he grew older, Montezuma began to develop deeper ties to the reservation at Fort McDowell, Arizona, where his kinsmen now lived. His attacks on the Indian Office, which had always condemned the government's authoritarian ways, came to be mixed with sympathy for Indian communities that needed support for development and protection from hostile neighbors. Gradually he shifted his focus accordingly, and even petitioned the hated agency to enroll him as a member of the Fort McDowell community.*

Montezuma came to argue that Indians should be freed from authoritarian control and encouraged to develop their distinctive talents and abilities. He never worked out the contradictions in his position: He believed the Indian Office was incapable of providing such encouragement, but implied in his writing that even though the government agency's efforts had been a failure, some source of assistance nonetheless would be needed. In the early 1920s, when he was diagnosed with tuberculosis, Montezuma brought his career full circle by returning to the Southwest, spending his last days with his relatives there. He died at Fort McDowell in January 1923.

The following excerpt from an essay published in the Society of American Indians' Quarterly Journal *in 1914 reveals Montezuma at his most outspoken. Written before his break with the SAI and his final return to Arizona, it contains an unrelenting attack on the Indian Office. At the same time, however, there is more here than a call for Indians to simply make their way on their own or perish. Montezuma did not echo the callous officials who spoke of "making room for the white man," but he did believe that Native tribes should be free to develop independently. His essay contains words of admiration for his Yavapai relatives and a clear sense that Indians are a "people" who have a right to survive. Note that Montezuma did not address the question of how—or if—American society should provide for that survival.*

We must free ourselves. Our peoples' heritage is freedom. Freedom reigned in their whole make-up. They harmonized with nature and lived accordingly. Preaching freedom to our people on reservations does not make them free any more than you can, by preaching, free those prisoners who are in the penitentiary. Reservations are prisons where our people are kept to live and die, where equal possibilities, equal education and equal responsibilities are unknown. . . .

We must do away with the Indian Bureau. The reservation system has debarred us as a race from acquiring that knowledge to appreciate our property. The government after teaching us how to live without work has come to the conclusion "that the Indians are not commercialists" and, therefore, "we (his guardian) will remove them as we think best and use them as long as our administration lasts and make friends."[1] The Indian Department has drifted into commercialism at the expense of our poor benighted people. So they go on and say, "Let us not allot those Indians on that sweet flowing water because there are others who will profit by damming it up and selling it out to the newcomers; that the Indians do not use or develop their lands; five acres of irrigated land is all that one Indian can manage, but in order to be generous, we will give him ten acres and close up the books and call it square; that their vast forest does them no good, before the Indian can open his eyes let us transfer it to the Forestry Reserve Department. Never mind, let the Indian scratch for his wood to cook with and to warm himself in the years to come; that the Indians have no use for rivers, therefore, we will go into damming business and build them on their lands without their consent. Pay? No! Why should we?" They give us "C" class water instead of "A" class. They have got us! Why? Because we do not know the difference.

"In this valley the Indians have too much land. We will move them from where they have lived for centuries" (by Executive order in behalf of the coming settlers). Even if he had cultivated and claims more than that, we will allot that Indian only ten acres. If he rebels and makes trouble, we will put him in jail until he is ready to behave himself." This poor Indian may try to get an Indian friend to help him out of his predicament. But right there the Indian helper is balked by the Indian Department and is told he is not wanted on the reservation. When an Indian collects money from among his tribe to defray expenses to Washington and back in order to carry their complaints, and to be heard and considered in their rights, the superintendent with the aid of the Indian policeman takes this Indian, takes the

[1]Apparently these quotations are fictitious. Montezuma used them as rhetorical devices to make his point that the Indian Office cared little for its charges' welfare.

money away from him and gives back the money to those who contributed, put[s] him in jail and brands him as a grafter. . . .

The sooner the Government abolishes the Indian Bureau, the better it will be for we Indians in every way. The system that has kept
alive the Indian Bureau has been instrumental in dominating over
our race for fifty years. In that time the Indian's welfare has grown
to the secondary and the Indian Bureau the whole thing, and therefore a necessary political appendage of the government. It sends out
exaggerated and wonderful reports to the public in order to suck the
blood of our race, so that it may have perpetual life to sap your life, my
life and our children's future prospects. There are many good things
to say about the Indian Department. It started out right with our
people. It fed them, clothed them and protected them from going outside of the reservations. It was truly a place of refuge. Then they were
dominated by agents; now they are called superintendents. On the
reservation our people did not act without the consent of the Superintendent; they did not express themselves without the approval of
the Superintendent, and *they did not dare to think,* for that would
be to rival, to the Superintendent. Yesterday, today, our people are in
the same benighted condition. As Indians they are considered non-
entities. They are not anything to themselves and not anything to the
world. . . .

We must be independent. When with my people for a vacation in
Arizona I must live outdoors; I must sleep on the ground; I must cook
in the fire on the ground; I must sit on the ground, I must eat nature's
food and I must be satisfied with inconveniences that I do not enjoy at
my Chicago home. Yet those blood relations of mine are independent,
happy, because they were born and brought up in that environment,
while as a greenhorn I find myself dependent and helpless in such
simple life. In order for we Indians to be independent in the whirl of
this other life, we must get into it and used to it and live up to its
requirements and take our chances with the rest of our fellow creatures. Being caged up and not permitted to develop our facilities has
made us a dependent race. We are looked upon as hopeless to save
and hopeless to do anything for ourselves. The only Christian way,
then, is to leave us alone and let us die in that condition. The conclusion is true that we will die that way if we do not hurry and get out of
it and hustle for our salvation. Did you ever notice how other races
hustle and bustle in order to achieve independence? Reservations
Indians must do the same as the rest of the wide world.

As a full-blooded Apache Indian[3] I have nothing more to say. Figure out your responsibility and the responsibility of every Indian that hears my voice.

[3]Montezuma, a Yavapai, regularly referred to himself as an Apache, perhaps because that tribe was better known to the public.

Arthur C. Parker Indicts the Government for Its Actions
1915

While serving as editor of the Society of American Indians' Quarterly Journal, *Seneca anthropologist Arthur Parker was asked to speak out on a wide variety of issues. Nevertheless, as a scholar and a member of an eastern tribe, he was more inclined to focus on education than the specific policies of the Indian Office. The following excerpt from the* Quarterly Journal *is an exception. In it Parker vents some of the frustration he felt over the ignorance and self-satisfaction that characterized so many lawmakers and government bureaucrats in the first decades of the twentieth century. While Parker did not share Carlos Montezuma's conviction that the Indian Office should be abolished, this essay presents a withering critique of the government's failed policies and stated good intentions. It offers his readers a sharp retort to the conventional view that the Indians' greatest problem was their own backwardness.*

There is little understanding of the blight that has fallen upon the red race within the United States. Notwithstanding the immense effort that is put forth by missionary bodies and by the federal government to remedy the unhappy situation of the Indians, neither of these forces acts as if it surely knew the elements with which it was dealing. But between the church and the state, if a comparison were drawn, the church understands better and responds more intelligently to the vital necessities of the race because its concern is with the man and not his

Arthur C. Parker, "Certain Important Elements of the Indian Problem," *Quarterly Journal,* 3 (1915): 24–38.

property. Even so, there is no clearly defined philosophy that reveals causes and points out remedies.

The Indian Bureau of the Interior Department is charged by Congressional action with dealing with Indian affairs. Like some vast machine bulky with many ill-fitting, or inferior parts it grinds on, consuming large sums of money for fuel and lubrication. Its constituted purpose is the protection of Indian property, the transformation of a race by civilization and its education, to the end that the Indians may become good citizens. Yet the Bureau is not achieving as great a measure of success as its Commissioner and earnest officials might wish. . . .

Neither the church nor the state with all its powers for organization, however, proceeds as if it had discovered why its task was so greatly hampered or why it must apply so much unproductive effort. It appears that the Indians are perverse, are naturally inclined to degradation, are inferior and unmindful as a race, or that they were an accursed people as some of the early colonists thought. Yet both church and state labor on for they feel that Providence has entrusted a benighted people to their keeping. Each factor is an instrument of American civilization, the one a civic power, the other a moral force. Each sees the Indian problem through standards of its own race. Each translates its conception of the needs of the Indian in terms of its own liking. Each understands through its own system of thinking, and bases its acts upon the sure assumption of its correctness. No attempt is ever made to outline the plan of its action and to explain why it thinks thus and so, and to submit such a plan to a psychologist, a sociologist, or an ethnologist for criticism and suggestion. Each has more or less definitely expressed the idea of the "white man's burden," or the obligation of American civilization and of Anglo-Saxon blood to lead mankind to higher goals. . . .

For the sake of definiteness and to stimulate constructive argument we wish to lay down seven charges, out of perhaps many more, that the Indian makes at the bar of American justice. Whether the white man believes them just or not, true or not, he cannot discharge his obligation to the red man until he considers them and understands that the Indian makes them because he at least feels them just charges. There will be white Americans who will see the charges as rightfully made and there will no doubt be some Indians, who, trained in the philosophies of the narrow school of the conqueror, will not admit them.

But notwithstanding objections we desire to submit the charges. The

Indians' view must be known if his sight is to be directed to broader visions.

The Charge against American Civilization

The people of the United States through their governmental agencies, and through the aggression of their citizens have:

1. Robbed a race of men—the American Indian—of their intellectual life;
2. Robbed the American Indian of his social organization;
3. Robbed the American Indian of his native freedom;
4. Robbed the American Indian of his economic independence;
5. Robbed the American Indian of his moral standards and of his racial ideals;
6. Robbed the American Indian of his good name among the peoples of the earth;
7. Robbed the American Indian of a definite civic status.

Each of the factors we have named is an essential to the life of a man or a nation. Picture a citizen of this republic without freedom, intellectual or social life, with no ability to provide his own food and clothing, having no sure belief in an Almighty being, no hero to admire and no ideals to foster, with no legal status and without a reputable name among men. Picture a nation or a people so unhappy. Yet civilization has conspired to produce in varying degrees all these conditions for the American Indians.

So much for the seven great robberies of the race. We have not even cared to mention the minor loss of territory and of resources—these are small things indeed, compared with the other thefts.

But though robbery has been committed, the Government and great citizens will exclaim, "We have given much to atone for your loss, brother red man."

Let us examine the nature of these gifts. The Federal Government and the kind hearts of friends have—

1. Given reserved tracts of land where Indians may live unmolested;
2. Given agents and superintendents as guardians and constituted a division of the Interior Department as a special bureau for the protection of the red race;
3. Given schools with splendid mechanical equipment;

4. Given the ignorant and poor, clerks who will think and act for them, and handle their money;
5. Given food, and clothing and peace;
6. Given new civilization;
7. Given a great religion.

So great and good gifts must have a price, for men cannot have these boons without suffering some disability. Measures are necessary to protect the Government itself from the results of its own charity and leniency to a people but lately regarded as enemies. The Government, therefore, as a price has—

1. Denied the Indians a voice in their own affairs to such an extent that Indian councils may not now meet without the consent of the Commissioner of Indian Affairs;
2. Denied the Indians the stimulus that springs from responsibility;
3. Denied the Indians the right to compete on the same terms as other men;
4. Denied the Indian a definition of his status in the country;
5. Denied the Indian the right to submit his claims against the United States in the Court of Claims, without special consent of Congress;
6. Denied the Indian a true and adequate education;
7. Denied the Indian the right to be a man, as other men of America are.

To be sure, the Indians were not at once denied these fundamental rights of human beings living in an organized civilized community. It was only as the seven great robberies became more or less complete and the reservation system grew, that the seven great denials took effect. The robberies and the denials are of a subtle psychological character and many there are who will ingeniously argue that the Indians still have all the things we have mentioned, or may have them if they will to do it, and that the seven gifts are but the gratuities of a charitable government. . . .

The result of such denials of basic human rights to proud men and women is definite and deep. Whether he can express his thoughts in words or not, whether the turmoil in his heart finds voice or not, every American Indian who has suffered this oppression that is worse than death feels that civilization has—

1. Made him a man without a country;
2. Usurped his responsibility and right of acting;

3. Demeaned his manhood;
4. Destroyed his ideals;
5. Broken faith with him;
6. Humiliated his spirit;
7. Refused to listen to his petitions.

The old reservation Indian feels all these things, and they burn into his very soul leaving him unhappy and dispirited. . . .

If these statements seem to tinge of irony or invective to the civilized man with the moral blind spot, they are, nevertheless, very real things to the Indian who knows wherein he is wounded. To him this analysis will seem mild indeed for it speaks nothing of a thousand deeds that made the four centuries of contact years of cruel misunderstanding. Yet, to him these earlier years were better years than now, for he was then a free man who could boast a nation, who could speak his thought and who bowed to no being save God, his superior and guardian. Nor will we here mention the awful wars against Indian women and children, the treacherous onslaughts on sleeping villages, the murders of the old and helpless, broken promises, the stolen lands, the robbed orphans and widow, done by men professing civilization and religion—for this is aside from our argument. We mention what is more awful than the robbery of lands, more hideous than the scalping and burning of Indian women and babies, more harrowing than tortures at the stake; we mean the crushing of a noble people's spirit and the usurpation of its right to be responsible, self supporting and self governing. . . .

The Restitution of the Seven Stolen Rights

The people of the United States through the Congress, through the Indian Bureau and through the activities of its conscientious citizenship must return to the Indian:

1. *An Intellectual Life.* In his native state the Indians had things to think about. These things in their several subjects were a part of his organized mental and external activities. . . . *Human beings have a primary right to an intellectual life, but civilization swept down upon groups of Indians and blighted or banished their intellectual life and left scattered groups of people mentally confused. . . .* The Indian must have his thought world given back.

2. *Social Organization.* The Indians were always fond of mingling together. They had many councils and conferences. They had associations, societies, fraternities and pastimes. These things grew out of

their social needs and each organization, game, dance, feast or custom filled some social need. . . . *Civilization has not done its part until every Indian again finds a definite setting and an active part in the organized activities of communities of men. . . .*

3. *Economic Independence.*   In his native state the Indian needed no government warehouse wherein to contain his food and clothing, he needed no mills in New York to make his blankets, no plantations in Brazil to furnish his breakfast drink, no laboratory in Detroit to decant his medical extracts. Each Indian tribe, and to a large extent each individual was a master of his own resources. They could procure, cultivate or make their life necessities. . . . *When the hunting grounds were diminished and the Indians driven upon small barren tracts they became dependent* for food, dishes, tools and clothing, *upon an external source. . . . From a self supporting people they had become abject paupers. . . .*

4. *The Right of Freedom.*   The first and greatest love of the American Indian was his freedom. Freedom had been his heritage from time immemorial. The red man by nature cannot endure enforced servitude or imprisonment. By nature he is independent, proud and sensitive. Freedom to the red man is no less sweet, no less the condition of life itself than to other men. . . .

5. *The God of Nations.*   The American Indian must have restored to him moral standards that he can trust. A weak and hypocritical Christianity will make the red man of today what his ancestors never were—an atheist. . . .

The red man as he is today more than even he himself realizes, needs to know God. The basis of all his ancient faith was God. To him God was the beginning and the end of all human experience. Though he could not comprehend the deity, he could revere him as the Great Mystery, whose all-seeing eye looked upon his every act.

Civilization through its churches and mission agencies must restore the Indian to a knowledge of his Maker. *Civilization through its schools must give back the red man great ideals over which he may map his life and by which he may build his character.*

6. *The Right of an Assured Status.*   Who is the Indian? What is he in the eyes of the law? The legal status of the Indian has never been defined. He is not an alien, he is not a foreigner, he is not a citizen. . . .

A group of people whose civic status is insecure becomes demoralized and the panic-spirit spreads to the individual. This fact is understood by thoughtful students of human progress.

7. *A Good Name among Nations.*   No race of men has been more unjustly misrepresented by popular historians than the American Indian. Branded as an ignorant savage, treacherous, cruel and immoral in his inmost nature, the Indian has received little justice from the ordinary historian whose writings influence the minds of school children. . . .

A great nation like the United States needs not to vilify the history of its aborigines. They were men and brave men. Their cruelty and treachery was no more than that of the white men. They fought and each deed of violence they committed as "ignorant savages" can be matched by more revolting deeds committed by "educated, civilized men." . . .

Why not stand with Wendell Phillips[1] and say to all the world,

"From Massachusetts Bay back to their own hunting grounds, every few miles is written down in imperishable record as the spot where the scanty, scattered tribes made a stand for justice and their right. Neither Greece, nor Germany nor France, nor the Scotch can show a prouder record. . . . The future will recognize it as a glorious record of a race that never melted out and never died, but stood up manfully, man by man, foot by foot, and fought it out for the land God gave him." . . .

The End of the Old Life and the Hope of the New

. . . If the church and the state are sincere in their desire to bring moral and civic salvation to the American Indian each must manfully face the conditions that has made the red man a problem. The psychological character of the problem must be recognized, for most of the red man's woes are diseases of mental attitude. The miseries of his external life are the results of a bewildered, dispirited and darkened mind. The work of the agencies of good is to give order and hope, incentive and ambition, education and ideals. Every effort of the Federal Government should be directed to these ends, and men must be made to feel the thrill of manhood, the joy of having a part in the making of their country, and a sure faith in Him who holds all mankind in the hollow of His hand.

If our argument has seemed harsh it has only been so as all truth is hard that awakens men to a point where the truth is perceived, for it is

---

[1] *Wendell Phillips* (1811–1884), a Boston lawyer, was a radical abolitionist who continued to agitate for social reform after the Civil War. In the 1870s and 1880s he spoke out in favor of women's suffrage, temperance, prison reform, and the fair treatment of Native Americans.

our belief that if we would atone our injury to a suffering man we must see his trouble as he sees it, though it pricks our conscience and causes us renewed effort.

The Society of American Indians Supports Tribal Claims

1913

While they endorsed the broad outlines of the government's educational program for Indians and accepted the notion that Native Americans would become a part of the American citizenry, members of the Society of American Indians did not share white America's assumption that Indian tribes were doomed to disappear. In part this reflected their own life histories. Francis La Flesche lived in Washington, D.C., but he continued to think of the Missouri valley as his home and of the Omaha as his tribe. Montezuma's poignant return to Arizona to die among his Yavapai relatives and Charles Eastman's return to the Canadian woods where he had spent part of his youth are only two of many examples of how sophisticated, urban Indians maintained their allegiance to their tribal heritage.

Tribal lawsuits aimed at winning compensation for damages inflicted by crooked agents or high-handed bureaucrats brought Progressive Era Indians' loyalty to tribe and faith in American institutions sharply into focus. It seemed perfectly reasonable to the members of the SAI that tribes who had been swindled or injured in the past should be able to present their grievances in a court of law. For years whites had sued the federal agencies in the U.S. Court of Claims for damages arising from government action or inattention; why not accord Indians the same right? The sticking point for government officials was the fact that the suits Indian groups contemplated were being brought on behalf of tribes the federal government was determined to eradicate. How could the Indian Office spend countless dollars "civilizing" the Lakota, officials might reason, trying to transform them from hunters to farmers, while allowing a lawsuit that might return ownership of the Black Hills to them? Officials might point out as well that the Lakota, the group suing for the return of the Black Hills, were now living on several reservations and were technically

---

Legal Aid Committee, "An Appeal to the Nation," *Quarterly Journal*, 1 (1913): 351–8.

no longer a recognized tribe. Reservation agents were adamant in their opposition to tribal claims because the very act of bringing suit offered local leaders a fresh and appealing forum from which they could claim legitimacy. In an age when reservation superintendents were working hard to undermine the authority of traditional chiefs, tribal lawsuits promised to legitimize indigenous leaders.

According to federal law, tribes could not sue the United States without congressional approval. As the twentieth century began, dozens of tribes began petitioning Washington officials for this permission. Many of the earliest plaintiffs were Oklahoma groups attempting to recover damages associated with land openings in what had been Indian Territory. Before long, the idea that tribes could win some monetary payment for treaty violations or unconscionable government actions had spread north and west, to the Great Lakes and the Plains. This expanding interest was fueled by attorneys eager to represent groups with worthy claims and by young, and generally well-educated, tribal members. It is not surprising that the Society of American Indians, a group led by educated Indians familiar with the law and federal policy, would take up the issue of tribal claims relatively early in its history.

The following appeal to the American public demonstrates the SAI's twin commitments to "justice" and the tribes. Because the society was officially committed to the ultimate integration of Native Americans into the larger society, it was not clear what its position would be regarding the long-term status of tribal societies. Nevertheless, this statement clearly supports those who were seeking the right to sue. The SAI saw no harm in allowing tribal groups to do so. The statement contains the text of a bill to allow tribal suits. The bill's declared purpose was to authorize "any nation, tribe, or band of Indians to submit claims against the United States," and it laid out procedures to be followed. Striking a pose of moral rectitude, this statement placed the enforcement of legal principles—fairness, justice—over loyalty to Indian Office policies. The society's appeal was not successful, but tribes persisted and the number of claims proliferated. Congress finally acted in 1946 when it created a special tribunal, the Indian Claims Commission, to adjudicate Native complaints.

A Great Injustice

Many American Indians believe that they have large claims against the government of the United States, and at the same time they have no opportunity to test their claims, except by appeal to Congress, which body has neither the time nor machinery adequate to handle promptly such a mass of legal material. The anomalous status or lack of status of the Indians in the courts of the country complicates the situation. Thus it happens that, year after year, decade after decade, the tribes wait for the relief that comes not. Bitterness is piled upon bitterness. The student of Indian affairs, the leaders in Indian administration and the informed statesmen in Congress have for many years cried out for some efficient remedy for this distressing, even disastrous, situation. One by one they have wearied in their efforts and almost abandoned hope. But the Society of American Indians believes that the failures of the past have been based on the lack of general and widespread information either in Congress or out. . . . Surely a great nation of one hundred million people can afford to do justice to the remnant of that race which once ruled our domain from shore to shore. Surely such a nation can trust the settlement of claims against itself in its own high courts.

No nation can afford to withhold justice; no nation can afford to delay justice in its relations with any people. How, then, can this nation, the self-constituted guardian of the Indian race, refuse aught of justice to its wards? While the nation delays, the Indian suffers, ofttimes in estate, always in mind. The rankling sense of injustice is a bar to progress. Worse than poverty is a vain hope for property. Until the matter is settled the Indian will wait, will stand still. That generally means he will sink down hill. . . .

The Remedy

. . . All the property claims against the United States government, whether they should prove to amount to fifty or even one hundred in number, should be given a prompt hearing and a final disposition. With them out of the way another remedy or method will be at hand for the solution of the next large group of legal problems.

The remedy is a simple one. *Open the United States Court of Claims to Indian tribes and groups.* There are, of course, many possible dangers involved in such a plan. Unless the measure adopted by Congress is carefully safeguarded, it will prove a source of new evils. The just settlement of the claims must be made as nearly certain as possible. The procedure should be made as inexpensive as possible for the Indian litigants. Exorbitant attorneys' fees should not be tolerated. No private fortune should come out of either Indian or government hands to attorneys concerned in the case.

Provisions of the Bill

. . . In brief, the measures proposed will open the United States Court of Claims to suits against the United States by Indian tribes, nations and bands. Such suits or claims based on facts, happening prior to the passage of the act, however, must be filed within five years after the passage of the act or be forever thereafter barred. The tribes or bands may file their petitions through attorneys, but the contracts between the Indians and any attorney must be approved by the Secretary of the Interior and the Commissioner of Indian Affairs in office at the time of the filing of the suit, before the attorney shall be permitted to represent the Indians in the Court of Claims.

The awards made by the court are to be paid out of any unappropriated funds in the hands of the Treasurer of the United States. The fees of the attorneys are to be such as the court shall fix as reasonable, but not to exceed the amount stipulated in the approved contract, and are to be met out of any sum or sums recovered in the suit and from no other source, unless so provided in the approved contract. The rights of the Indians are not to be withheld by reason of the usual statutes of limitation, since the Indians have not previously been competent to bring their claims before the court, and all treaties, papers, correspondence and records of the United States are made accessible to the attorneys. If not satisfied, either party may appeal to the Supreme Court of the United States. The bill opens the door for a thorough and honest determination of the matters at issue between the government and its wards.

The Bill

Authorizing any nation, tribe or band of Indians to submit claims against the United States to the Court of Claims with the right of either party to appeal to the Supreme Court of the United States.

Be it enacted by the Senate and House of Representatives of the United States of America in Congress assembled, That all claims of whatsoever nature which any nation, tribe, or band of Indians may have against the United States, which have not heretofore been determined by the Court of Claims, may be submitted to the Court of Claims, with the right of appeal to the Supreme Court of the United States by either party, for the determination of the amount, if any, due either or any of said nations, tribes, or bands from the United States under any treaties, agreements or laws of Congress or for the misappropriation of any of the funds of either or any of the said nations, tribes or bands, or for the failure of the United States to pay either or any of the said nations, tribes, or bands any money or other property due; and jurisdiction is hereby conferred upon the Court of Claims, with the right of either party to appeal to the Supreme Court of the United States, to hear and determine all legal and equitable claims, if any, of said nations, tribes or bands, or any of them against the United States, and to enter judgment thereon. Provided, That all claims based on fact, happening before the passage of this Act shall be forever barred unless suit is brought thereon within five years after the passage of this Act.

Sec. 2.   That if any claim or claims be submitted to said courts they shall settle the rights therein, both legal and equitable, of each and all the parties thereto, notwithstanding lapse of time or statutes of limitation, and any payment which may have been made upon any claim so submitted may be pleaded as an offset in such suits or actions. * * *[1] The claim or claims of each nation, tribe, or band may be presented separately or jointly by petition, subject, however, to amendment; and such action shall make the petitioner or petitioners party plaintiff or plaintiffs and the United States party defendant and any nation, tribe, or band, the court may deem necessary to a final determination of such suit or suits may be joined therein as the court may order. Such petition shall set forth all the facts on which the claims for recovery are based, and the said petition may be signed by the attorney for the petitioning nation, tribe, or band, and shall be verified by him after examination of the records pertaining to the claim or claims, and no other verification shall be necessary. Official letters, papers, documents, and public records, or certified copies thereof, may be used in evidence and the departments of the government shall give access to the attorney or attorneys of the said nations, tribes, or bands of Indians to such treaties, papers, correspondence, and the records as may be needed by the attorney or attorneys for said nations, tribes, or bands of Indians.

Sec. 3.   *That upon the final determination of such suit, cause or action in favor of the nation, tribe, or band, the Court of Claims shall decree that the Secretary of the Treasury shall place to the credit of the said nation, tribe, or band the amount found due to the nation, tribe or band.*

Sec. 4.   That upon the final determination of such suit, cause or

---

[1]The Legal Aid Committee deleted sections of the bill they considered inappropriate and added other sections (marked with italics) they felt were needed. The purpose of these changes was to ensure the prompt payment of claims.

action, the Court of Claims shall decree such fees as it shall find reasonable to be paid the attorney or attorneys employed therein by each of said nations, tribes, or bands of Indians, under contracts negotiated and approved, as provided by existing law, and in no case shall the fee decreed by said Court of Claims be in excess of the amounts stipulated in the contracts approved by the Commissioner of Indian Affairs *holding office at the date of filing the claim* and the Secretary of the Interior, and no attorney shall have a right to represent or shall represent any nation, tribe, or band of Indians in any suit, cause, or action under the provisions of this Act until his contract shall have been approved as herein provided. The fees decreed by the court to the attorney or attorneys of record shall be paid out of any sum or sums recovered in such suits or actions, and no part of such fee shall be taken from any money in the Treasury of the United States belonging to such nations, tribes, or bands of Indians in whose behalf the suit was brought, unless specifically authorized in the contract approved by the Commissioner of Indian Affairs and the Secretary of the Interior as herein provided.

The Great Justice

The bill is designed simply as a tool of justice, framed by unselfish men, to promote the ends of justice. Why, in a nation funded on the principles of equality, should justice be so far removed from the Indian? In former days, when the tribes were strong in number, the Indian did not hesitate to go to war openly with any whom he thought deprived him of his rights. But now, weakened in numbers and subdued by the white man's law, he perforce must wait upon the slow machinery of legislation and postponed judicial decisions, cursed, ofttimes, by "his dream of getting twenty-five cents out of some stale claim, instead of earning twenty-five dollars by devoting the same to work." . . .[1]

The Society of American Indians makes its appeal to the American people. We realize that Congress will heed the call of the nation. We believe that Congress desires to deal justly, but Congress has many things to do. . . .

Our appeal is not for favor, but for simple justice, your own justice, the justice of your own courts. A proud people will ask no more; a worthy nation will grant no less.

[1]The statement is apparently that of an unnamed critic of the claims process.

5

Popular Images of Indians: Cartoons and Commentary, 1913–1916

In the early twentieth century, Native American activists and writers occasionally took the time to comment on popular notions of Indianness. The documents reprinted in this chapter contain a few of these statements. They reflect a growing willingness on the part of Native Americans to respond to public comments and to argue with those who presented themselves as "experts."

Cartoons from the Quarterly Journal
1913–1916

Most of these cartoons were drawn by non-Indians and published first in popular newspapers. (Unfortunately it has so far not been possible to identify the artists who drew these reprinted cartoons or to locate the publications where they first appeared, although every effort has been made to do so.) What makes these drawings interesting "Indian" documents is that they were reprinted in the Society of American Indian's Quarterly Journal *with comments supplied by the editor. If not "Indian" cartoons, they are nonetheless "Indian-endorsed" drawings placed in the* Journal *to make a specific point. It is not clear whether the drawings from the* Quarterly Journal *itself were created by Indians or non-Indians.*

"Lo, the Poor Indian! Whose Untutored Mind Sees Grafters on Both Sides, Before, Behind," 1913.

Published in the same issue as the "Appeal to the Nation" on the land claims issue (see chapter 4), this cartoon illustrated the interests that appeared when Indians tried to manage their money or resources. An attorney, a "man higher up" in a tree, even a dog, appear for their share. "Only education, a definite legal status and high personal honor can save the Indian so affected," the *Journal* declared.

Quarterly Journal, 1 (1913): 85.

"If We Must Have a Statue to the Indian in New York Harbor, Why Not Have Something Appropriate Like This?" 1913.

Initiated by a groundbreaking ceremony on February 22, 1913, that was attended by dozens of aging tribal chiefs and President William Howard Taft, the National Indian Memorial was designed to dominate the entrance to New York City. A hundred-foot-high bronze warrior would hold up his hand in a sign of peace, welcoming newcomers to America. The memorial was the brain-child of department store heir Rodman Wanamaker; it made for a dramatic groundbreaking ceremony but was never built. Noted the editors of the *Journal:*

> The irony of building a gigantic statue to a race of men who have been so grossly injured by the evils of civilization can not but be apparent to those who think even superficially. The idea of the statue, however, is a noble one, and it is to be hoped that it will correctly portray the tribes that welcomed and nursed the feeble colonists. The cartoonist thinking over this matter has pictured the way the Indian has been rewarded all too frequently for demanding his rights in his own country.

Quarterly Journal, 1 (1913): 85.

"Lo, the Poor Indian!" 1913.

The editors of the *Journal* saw in this cartoon an image of the Indians' fate so long as their lives were managed by government officials:

> The Indian whose arm is bound by the broken shield of government neglect may cast aside that shield when he will be asserting his independence as an individual and taking up the sword of individual action. He is still an Indian but a transformed one and one who has found that adjustment to conditions and an active struggle alone can save him.

Quarterly Journal, 1 (1913): 86.

"The Progressive Indian American," 1913.

This image of success was intended to counter the stereotypical representations in other cartoons. It is interesting that the editors identify this image as someone who belongs to a distinct race. Like Arthur Parker, who defended the special gifts and needs of the Indian race in his editorial "Certain Important Elements of the Indian Problem" (see chapter 4), this cartoon promoted the notion that people could be both "civilized" and "Indian" at the same time:

> This man is not less an Indian because he has discovered the secret of success as an American in his own country. It is such Indians who best understand the needs of their people and who can help them most. . . . You will find an emblem in the coat lapel of this man. . . . It makes him a part of a great race movement and gives him a standing as a factor in the welfare of his race and a builder of a better humanity.

Quarterly Journal, 1 (1913): 87.

"How Shall the Red Man's Loyalty Be Rewarded?" 1914.

This cartoon was reprinted as a comment on the efforts to win tribes a hearing before the U.S. Court of Claims, as well as on the SAI's campaign to win a universal grant of citizenship for all Indians. The editors noted, "Hundreds of loyal Indians fought in the Revolutionary War, more in the War of 1812.... Thousands fought in the Civil War.... hundreds were in the Spanish war.... The Indian now appeals for standing and voice in the court of Claims; he asks for a definition of his status in this home land of his and for a codification of the Indian law.... Shall he again be turned away?"
Quarterly Journal, 2 (1914): 165.

"Expectation and Reality," 1916.

The editors of the *American Indian Magazine* (the *Quarterly Journal* was renamed in 1916) could not resist reprinting this commentary on the public's ignorance regarding American Indians. It was published following the Society of American Indians' annual conference, held in Cedar Rapids, Iowa, in September 1916.

Our annual conferences always disappoint the man who has a set belief that the Indian is incapable of civilization. Expecting to see a wondrous display of gaudy blankets and plumed bonnets, the Ordinary Citizen rubs his hands and conjures up the pseudo-Indian words he knows. He gets as far as "Ugh" and "Heap" and then wonders if it will be safe to take the family along to see the pow-wow.

Then the Indians come. There is a welcome meeting at the university and the Ordinary Citizen goes to see the Wild Indians half expecting to see an escort of the militia and Buffalo Bill in charge. And what does the Ordinary Citizen see? Why, just plain folks, Indians to be sure, but looking like other Americans. Then he gets a jolt. "They don't want scalps—they just want to be plain, ordinary citizens and to be as free as other United Staters!" The ordinary citizen gets a deal of education when he meets with the Indians at the university, and he's their friend forever after.

American Indian Magazine, 14 (1916): 225.

Chauncey Yellow Robe
on the Wild West Shows
1914

The practice of non-Indians displaying Indians in traditional garb began in 1492 when Christopher Columbus captured some of the Arawak he encountered in the Caribbean and carried them back to the Spanish court. Throughout the colonial era, Indian delegations never failed to cause a sensation in Europe. It was not until the nineteenth century, however, that displays of Indians reached a mass audience. The principal American publicist of Indians and Indianness at mid-century was George Catlin, a Philadelphia artist who toured his gallery of paintings—which he claimed had all been rendered from life—across Europe. Catlin's images (sometimes supplemented on tour with living Native people) depicted Indian life on the American Plains. His canvases, which brought viewers face-to-face with buffalo hunters, painted warriors, and Natives in colorful costumes, gave viewers a vicarious thrill and helped create a market for the work of less talented authors and illustrators.

After the Civil War, thousands of dime novels and traveling theatrical reviews fed the public's continuing appetite for dramatic displays of Indian life, but the next innovation, one that would affect Indians directly, was the creation in 1883 of Buffalo Bill's "Wild West Show." Part circus, part ethnographic display, and part self-promoting stage play, founder William F. Cody's extravaganza employed dozens of Indians who rode, shot, and whooped their way around arenas throughout

Chauncey Yellow Robe, "The Menace of the Wild West Show," *Quarterly Journal,* 2 (1914): 224–5.

**Figure 11.
Chauncey
Yellow Robe
and Family.**
Proud of his affilia-
tion with Richard
Pratt and the
Carlisle School,
Chauncey Yellow
Robe spent his
entire career in the
Indian Service. His
post as disciplinar-
ian at the Rapid
City Boarding
School made him
an important go-
between for Indian
families and gov-
ernment officials.
Yellow Robe is pic-
tured here with his
wife and two
daughters.
Photo courtesy of
South Dakota State
Historical Society—
State Archives.

*Europe and the United States. They and their imitators held the public's
interest for more than thirty years, losing their grip only after motion pictures established themselves as the preeminent form of mass entertain-
ment during World War I.*

    *Because Cody presented his shows as educational, and because the
public embraced them so enthusiastically, only a few people criticized*

them. Missionaries resented the shows' celebration of "heathenism," and government agents disliked the way Cody's Indians were free to ignore Indian Office regulations as they traveled happily about the country. The public ignored these concerns as it flocked to see sham battles between cavalrymen and warriors and the recreated heroics of former U.S. Army scout Cody.

In the document reprinted below, Chauncey Yellow Robe offers a different view of the Wild West shows. Yellow Robe (1870–1930), whose mother was a niece of Sitting Bull, spent his early childhood in South Dakota but was sent to Carlisle while still in grammar school. The athletic young Sioux was an enthusiastic student. He became cadet captain at the school in 1892. That same year he led the Carlisle contingent in the Chicago parade to honor the four hundredth anniversary of the first Columbus voyage. Following his graduation from Carlisle in 1895, Yellow Robe became the disciplinarian at the Indian boarding school in Rapid City, South Dakota.

One of the few Native American commentaries ever published on Wild West shows, Yellow Robe's statement was first delivered as a speech at the fourth annual meeting of the Society of American Indians in Madison, Wisconsin, in the fall of 1914 and then published in the society's Quarterly Journal. *In his speech, Yellow Robe attacked both the message of the shows and the public's apparently bottomless appetite for lurid views of Indian life. Yellow Robe remained a critic of Wild West shows for the rest of his life. In the 1920s, as movies became popular, he served as a consultant on films he believed were authentic. The best known of the films he worked on was* Silent Enemy, *released in 1929.*

... It is now more than four centuries since Columbus came to our shores and claimed the country and gave us the name of Indians, and at the same time inaugurated the first Indian show by importing some of the Indians across the water for exhibition before the Spanish throne, and to-day the practice continues to exist in the wild-west Indian shows.

Some time ago, Judge [Cato] Sells, the United States Commissioner of Indian Affairs, said: "Let us save the American Indian from the curse of whiskey." I believe these words hold the key to the Indian problem of to-day, but how can we save the American Indian if the Indian Bureau is permitting special privileges in favor of the wild-west Indian shows, moving-picture concerns, and fair associations for commercializing the

Indian? This is the greatest hindrance, injustice, and detriment to the present progress of the American Indians toward civilization. . . .

In some of the celebrations, conventions, and county fairs in Rapid City and other reservation border towns, in order to make the attraction a success, they think they cannot do without wild-west Indian shows, consequently certain citizens have the Indian show craze. . . . We can see from this state of affairs that the white man is persistently perpetuating the tribal habits and customs. We see that the showman is manufacturing the Indian plays intended to amuse and instruct young children and is teaching them that the Indian is only a savage being. We hear now and then of a boy or girl who is hurt or killed by playing savage. These are the direct consequences of the wild-west Indian shows and moving pictures that depict lawlessness and hatred.

Before the closing history of the nineteenth century an awful crime was committed in this great Christian nation. . . . A band of Sioux Indians, including women and children, unarmed, were massacred. The wounded were left on the field to die without care at Wounded Knee by the United States troops just because they had founded a new religion called "The Indian Messiah." This was a cowardly and criminal act without diplomacy. Twenty-three years afterward, on the same field of Wounded Knee, the tragedy was reproduced for "historical preservation" in moving picture films and called "The Last Great Battle of the Sioux." The whole production of the field was misrepresented and yet approved by the Government. This is a disgrace and injustice to the Indian race.

I am not speaking here from selfish and sensitive motives, but from my own point of view, for cleaner civilization, education, and citizenship for my race. . . .

Arthur C. Parker on the
Alleged Racial Inferiority of Indians
1914

The editor of the Quarterly Journal *aimed directly at the myth of a racial hierarchy in this column from late 1914. Using an editorial statement from* American Medicine *as a foil, Arthur Parker spoke to the popular idea that America was populated by fixed racial groups which were somehow "pure" and whose "mixture" would bring about social upheaval. Such thinking was popular among the eugenicists of Parker's day and was often cited by those who wished to limit immigration to the United States or restrict the citizenship rights of particular racial groups. The notion of a racial hierarchy had also been an essential element in much of recent federal Indian policy. Indians were sent to boarding schools, stripped of "surplus" lands, and subjected to missionization, the reasoning went, because they were part of a "backward" group.*

While some anthropologists were sympathetic to this racist outlook, Parker rejected it as unscientific and wrong. Citing the writings of Franz Boas, the Seneca scholar pointed out that "races" were relatively arbitrary groups of people which were difficult to define and which contained a wide variety of physical types. He also noted the many aspects of social circumstance — economic well-being, education, home life — that affected behavior, rejecting the link between "blood" and human personality. Like Boas, who opposed immigration restriction based on the national origins of immigrants, Parker argued that environment, not physical type or heredity, shaped behavior.

This brief essay demonstrates how readily the new generation of educated Indian leaders responded to simplistic attacks on their community. In an era when antimiscegenation laws restricted both African American and Indian marriages, Parker spoke out clearly about the myths of intermarriage. (He was, after all, the son of a Seneca chief and a white woman who had taught school on the Cattaraugus Reservation.) Parker emphasized that there was no evidence racial intermarriage was harmful and called those who defended white superiority "self-admiring egotists."

Arthur C. Parker, "Editor's Viewpoint," *Quarterly Journal*, 2 (1914): 261–8.

Indian Blood

The anthropologist is not worried over the fate of the red man's blood. It flows in thousands of the most vigorous citizens in America; yet the editor of *American Medicine* for September, 1914, is worried. He says that it must now be realized that "a physique evolved from savage life is somehow unfit to live in civilization." The Indians, he affirms, thrived under famine and privation, but with food protection and other good things the whites have given them they melt away. "The type is out of place and cannot be set back to an environment fit for it," says the editor who adds, "and perhaps, we cannot create an artificial one." The rate at which the Indian is merging his blood into the white race he apparently regards as alarming. Then he asks as to the nature of the damage and how it can be prevented. If it cannot be prevented, he asks whether the world will be the worse or if it will be better off for the extinction of the Indian. "Certain Irish types disappear from the population and no one seems to mind it," says the editor, "so why shed tears over a handful of Indians left behind by the progress of evolution of man and civilization? The fate of the mixed blood will probably be the same in spite of the apparent vigor of the present stock. Such hybrid types never have survived if the two parent types are widely different." . . .

We should like to say that the good doctor draws his conclusions from incomplete evidence and that he is apparently ignorant of several facts. Among the things we think he should consider are these: 1st, *not all* white men who married Indian women were or are abnormal. Some of the best European blood in the early days of exploration and colonization was left among the Indians of the Northwest, as a result of marriage mostly by tribal custom it may be true, but nevertheless, marriage. We do not believe the children of these unions were undesirable human beings. Neither were or are all white women who marry Indians, women who are deficient. The entire evil resulting from the blood union of the Indian and the white race comes directly and almost solely from its diseased, immoral, criminal and uneducated classes. A defective woman of either race having mixed blood children by a man below normal physical and moral standard is quite likely to find her issue quite as diseased and immoral as hereditary tendencies on both sides might indicate. But the legitimate marriage of moral and physically sound members of these two races may be expected to produce normal offspring. Subsequent environment usually determines the result. The mixed blood of normal parents does prosper, does live, and shall increasingly add to his country's greatness. Hundreds of men and women of more or less remote descent from the "old American stock" attest the truth of this assertion. . . .

American Indian blood is in America to stay. Though it becomes diffused as centuries weave on, its virtue shall live in the achievements of the proud men and women in whose arteries it flows.

Blood Mixture among Races

No race, as we know races, is an unmixed race. All so-called races are the result of mixtures. Food, soil, locality, climate, available materials, systems of thought, and dominant languages caused the development of the types of humanity when the various geographical areas were more or less isolated. Yet all groups of human beings since remote periods have received the influx of blood from others. The peoples of Europe terming themselves Caucasian are the result of mixtures of prehistoric elements as well as of later races. Europe received and absorbed mixtures of Asiatic and African peoples. Asia received the blood of Africans and Malays. Even the red men of America may have received, even after the crystallization of the race, the influx of Scandinavian, Malayan, and Mongolian blood. . . .

The "white" race is not uniformly white, but ranges from black to a yellow or florid "white," and an olive. This great Caucasian race, which in its many branches sprang from common ancestors, embraces (1) the north Europeans, Germans, Kurds, Afghans; (2) French, Welsh, Russians, Poles, Roumanans, Armenians, East Persians, Jews; (3) Iberians, Italians, Greeks, Berbers, Hindus, Dravideans, and Ainus; and many other stocks. Widely scattered is the red race of the Americas, diverse as are its languages and customs, the red race is far more stable and crystallized than this race of many mixtures, colors, and customs. . . .

We do not believe that the mixture of the great racial stocks has ever produced an inferior people or lessened human capacity. Clean blood of whatever stock is good human blood.

And so races continue to evolve, ever changing, ever intermixing, yet each one ever vainly sure it is of pure lineage and superior to other men. Humanity, or civilized humanity, if you please, will never realize or miss its mission until races come to understand their common ancestry and each will mingle with the other trustfully, without each dogmatically assuming its own right to thrust its culture upon the other, for race virtues and dogmas, like race bloods, are themselves not unmixed. . . .

Inferior or Only Different?

There is a school of race philosophy that propagates the idea that the blonde Aryan or white man is the destined ruler and civilizer of the World. A closer analysis would show that the theorists of this school are as a rule, self-admiring egotists, whose emotional nature is to say the least erratic.

Dr. Franz Boas, one of the greatest anthropologists, in a recent article in *Everybody's Magazine,* discusses this belief and states that it has no foundation in observed fact. He intimates that is merely a reflex of the dominant idea of the north European that he is a superior man by virtue of his blood and race. Very aptly he remarks: "This notion prevails among ourselves with equal force, for we shake our heads over the ominous influx of inferior races from eastern Europe. Inferior by heredity? No. Socially different? Yes; on account of the environment in which they have lived, and therefore different from ourselves . . ."

6

World War I

More than ten thousand Native American men served in World War I, nearly one-fourth of the eligible adult population. In 1917 and 1918, Indian "doughboys" from Arizona, Montana, New York, and elsewhere fought in every major battle from Château-Thierry to the Argonne Forest. These soldiers were not shunted off into secondary roles or, like African Americans, forced to serve in segregated units. In fact, Indian soldiers were frequently used as frontline scouts and especially praised for their bravery under fire. The exploits of Indian "warriors" were featured in press reports, and tales of Indian telephone operators who confused German eavesdroppers by communicating in tribal languages became a staple of battlefield folklore. As had been the case with the Irish in the American Civil War or with more recent immigrants in the Spanish-American conflict, World War I gave Native people an opportunity to participate in a great national drama, in the process linking their own ethnicity to a patriotic cause.

For the most part, American Indians welcomed the chance to serve in the war. Some 6,500 Native American men were drafted into the military, and at least another 3,500 enlisted. Requests for deferments were rare, despite the fact that many of the new soldiers were not yet citizens of the nation they were being called on to protect. In addition to providing soldiers to the military, the American Indian community collectively bought more than $25 million worth of war bonds (approximately $75 for every Native person in the country) and made substantial contributions to the Red Cross and other war-related charities. Many communities sent their soldiers off with elaborate ceremonies, supported them while they were away by planting victory gardens, and welcomed home survivors with dances and celebrations. Still, the irony of serving a nation that had dispossessed them, and of fighting to defend "democracy" when their own communities were ruled by the Indian Office, was not lost on Indian people. They understood the call to service, but they would insist on significant compensation for their effort.

The following documents present five Indian commentaries on World War I, demonstrating the accuracy of a recent scholar's assertion that the war years marked "a cultural watershed in modern Native American history."[1] First, writing in his newsletter, *Wassaja,* Carlos Montezuma argues that while Indians eager to serve should be allowed to do so, noncitizens should not be subject to the draft. He expressed the frustration many felt toward the government's insensitivity. Second, Chauncey Yellow Robe, the Carlisle graduate who had criticized Wild West shows, describes the "Indian patriotism" that fueled Native American participation in the war. His enthusiasm—and anti-German rhetoric—demonstrate how fervently some tribal leaders embraced the struggle against the Germans. Third and fourth, Charles Eastman and Zitkala Ša speak out at war's end. Like leaders of other colonized or conquered peoples around the globe, the two writers sought to link their group's aspirations to President Woodrow Wilson's call for a lasting peace based on the "self-determination" of peoples. Finally, Robert Yellowtail, a young Crow boarding school graduate who was a generation younger than the other writers, defends his tribe in terms that demonstrate how quickly Native politicians and writers grasped the implications of Wilson's rhetoric and America's victory. Testifying before Congress in the fall of 1919—as the battle over ratification of the Versailles treaty was reaching its peak—Yellowtail expresses his hope that the president will "not forget that within the boundaries of his own nation are the American Indians who have no rights whatsoever—not even the right to think for themselves."

[1]Thomas A. Britten, *American Indians in World War I: At Home and at War* (Albuquerque: University of New Mexico Press, 1997), 157.

Carlos Montezuma on the Draft

1917

Because he was outspoken on so many issues, it was not surprising that Montezuma issued a dramatic statement on the conscription of American Indians into the United States Army. Deeply distrustful of the government and opposed to the Indian Office's policies, Montezuma was among the sharpest critics of the draft. He believed Native Americans should seek out their own distinctive place in American life, free from government restrictions and popular prejudices. By the time America entered the war in April 1917, the Chicago physician had broken with the Society of American Indians and was publishing his own newsletter, Wassaja. *Montezuma held that a nation which would not grant citizenship to Indians should not expect Native Americans to sacrifice their lives to defend it.*

WASSAJA is not against the war nor against Indians going into the army if they so wish, of their own free will. But is it just to force them to be soldiers?

Aliens in the United States have a country of their origin. They enjoy the rights and privileges of the United States Government, as aliens are entitled. And it is no more than right to draft them into the army.

Can we not see that the Indians are wards in their dispossessed country, and they are not aliens? It looks as though they are without a country. One may say, "America is their country." If that is the case, they have not the rights and privileges of citizenship of the United States Government. They are not citizens. They have fewer privileges than have foreigners. They are wards of the United States of America without their consent or the chance of protest on their part. What does that mean? They are not capable of attending to their own affairs. They are not of age. They are classed as minors. Does it look right to force them into this war and thus increase our Christian injustice to them?

The other day a delegate of Indians, who had been to Washington to protest against the drafting of their young men into the army, called on WASSAJA. We asked the interpreter what the Chief told the Washington Father. He said, "The Chief said, 'If you give us *everything,* you can take my young men across the water to fight the Germans.'" By

Carlos Montezuma, "Drafting Indians and Justice," *Wassaja,* 2, no. 7 (October 1917): 3.

"give us everything" he clearly meant freedom from the oppression of the Indian Office and citizenship—that they might enjoy the rights and privileges thereof. That strikes the keynote of the Indian's contention. He wants "everything" that you have for himself—meaning citizenship. The Indian Office keeps us Indians from our rights. It tells the country that we are competent to be soldiers, but are not competent to be citizens. These Indians were told that a letter had been sent to their Superintendent stating that the Crow young men would be exempt from the draft.

Not many days after, Congress passed a bill to draft aliens, which no doubt included the Indians. WASSAJA does not know what Chief Plenty Coos[2] will think or say when he will be informed that Congress has passed a law to take his young men for war. Do you wonder that Indians lose faith in the Washington Father? The Indian has a soul and that is why we are seeking for our inherited rights. The Indian cannot believe contradictory statements; first, that his young men will not be taken from him to be made soldiers to fight in France and then, inside of ten days, that he will be informed that his young men WILL be taken to fight. Since we do not get "everything" from our Washington Father, we cannot see the justice of giving our strong young men to be killed.

We Indians are ready to defend the country of our forefathers as we have been doing these five hundred years against all odds, but what have we and what are we? We are nothing but wards; we are not citizens and we are without a country in this wide world. It is a sad picture that haunts America's conscience, and now worse than ever we are forced into the army, as though we were citizens or at least aliens. The wards are called upon to protect their Protectors! Has God given us Indians to the world to be used as tools, without justice? It is damnable to be an Indian!

WASSAJA believes that this drafting of the Indians into the army is another wrong perpetrated upon the Indian without FIRST bestowing his just title—THE FIRST AMERICAN CITIZEN. Why not? He was here before Columbus, he was here before Washington, he was here before Lincoln and he was here and you came. There is Justice. Is this justice?

The legislature at Washington and the people of the United States

[2]*Plenty Coups* (Alaxchiiaahush) (1848?–1932) was a Crow war leader who became one of the most prominent Indians of the early reservation era. He organized his followers to resist the government's most drastic intrusions into Crow life and he appeared often at national celebrations and meetings with government officials. While often referred to in the popular press as "Plenty Coos," the Montana chief was officially "Plenty Coups."

may be ignorant of the awful imposition in which we, as true Americans, are imprisoned and enslaved. But WASSAJA hopes that these words will stir up the patriotic feelings throughout these United States of America, so that his race will be freed from the bondage of the Indian Office and so that the Indians will be made citizens. Then, and only then, can this country proudly draft them so that they will march side by side under the same flag with the brave patriots to victory truly, then, in behalf of THEIR COUNTRY.

Chauncey Yellow Robe on the War Effort
1918

Speaking at the Society of American Indians' annual conference in Pierre, South Dakota, in 1918, Yellow Robe described the war in Europe as a struggle for freedom. He argued that Native Americans had long been defenders of freedom; thus, they naturally allied themselves with the American cause. As the leaders of many ethnic groups did in World War I (and as others had done in previous conflicts), Yellow Robe was careful to point out that the war proved once again how "American" Indian people were. Their bravery and loyalty set them apart from "German savagery." In his enthusiasm, Yellow Robe also embraced the supernationalism that spread across the country in response to the war. Aligning himself with the president and the armed forces, he took advantage of the war to criticize Germans and others who were currently being characterized as "un-American." Yellow Robe seemed to forget the hardships imposed on Indians as he extended his support not only to the war but also to the effort to "Americanize" European immigrants and bring them into "our glorious America."

... We know that the "Indian Patriotism" has always existed among the American Indians—as we see that they have demonstrated in this Great World War.

After the Discovery of America the Pilgrims came to our shores to seek for freedom in our native land, the red men have welcomed them

Chauncey Yellow Robe, "Indian Patriotism," *American Indian Magazine,* 6 (1919): 129–30.

with their right hand of fellowship on that famous "Plymouth Rock"—
the foundation of human liberty.

The American Indian has helped the white man to fight for the
"Declaration of Independence" and in every succeeding war since that
the Indian has sacrificed his blood under the emblem of the United
States.

More than a year ago when the United States entered upon this
world conflict for the principles of freedom and democracy, by patriotic motives thousands of American Indians have gone forth to answer
the call for service and now today they have engaged in every branch
of the war service, that there are millions of dollars they have invested
in the Liberty Bonds and thousands of dollars donated to the Red
Cross and the Y.M.C.A. services.

The American Indian is not lacking in patriotism, he is not a disloy-
alist—a slacker or a traitor, but is a true patriot.

The Indian—the native of America—has more right to fight for
freedom in this great war. Now we see that they are right in the thick-
est of the firing line, fighting the German savagery—sacrificing side
by side with the Allies on the great European battlefields to save the
world for civilization, freedom and democracy.

In this war we see that the Indian has demonstrated his bravery
and patriotism. At the battle front two American Indians—a lieutenant
and a private, were on scout duty, found their way through the German line several miles back and there they found a staff headquarter,
peeped through the window, the German officers smoking and drinking wine. The Indian scouts stepped back and threw their grenades
through the window, killed all but one trying to get out for help. Private Jas. Stiff Tail, one of the Indian scouts, drew out his revolver and
shot him dead. After this disturbance, both the Indian scouts were
wounded, yet they returned through the German line to the American
side and then back to the hospital, and there Private James Stiff Tail
was asked how he was. He said, "I am all right," and expired. The
noble deeds of these two Indians will go down in history. . . .

We, the American Indians, are not all dead, and we will fight on and
die fighting for this freedom.

We will not offer our "Pipe of Peace" to the Kaiser of Germany until
his government will be crushed and buried and the people of Germany will be freed under a new government and that the people of the
world will live under one unity, peace, liberty and democracy.

Within the last decade there are many millions of European emigrants that have landed in America—some having come from the

German Empire, colonizing among themselves within our borders, speaking their own language. They have no respect for our American laws and seek to Germanize America. The Germans and every other nationality colonization are dangerous—Un-American.

We must Americanize our glorious America under one government, one American language for all, one flag and one God.

Zitkala Ša on the Paris Peace Conference
1919

In 1916 Zitkala Ša (then writing as Gertrude Bonnin) returned to Washington to serve as secretary of the Society of American Indians. In 1918 she became editor of the organization's journal, which had changed its name to the American Indian Magazine. *While serving as editor she published articles that praised the Native American contributions to the war effort and called for the extension of citizenship to all Indians. With the war's end, however, she used the idealism of the moment and the sacrifice of Indian soldiers to press her case for a greater recognition of Native American issues.*

The eyes of the world are upon the Peace Conference sitting at Paris.

Under the sun a new epoch is being staged!

Little peoples are to be granted the right of self determination!

Small nations and remnants of nations are to sit beside their great allies at the Peace Table; and their just claims are to be duly incorporated in the terms of a righteous peace.

Paris, for the moment, has become the center of the world's thought. Divers[e] human petitions daily ascend to its Peace Table through foreign emissaries, people's representatives and the interest's lobbyists. From all parts of the earth, claims for adjustments equitable and otherwise are cabled and wirelessed. What patience and wisdom is needed now to render final decisions upon these highly involved and delicate enigmas reeking with inhumanities! The task

Gertrude Bonnin, "Editorial Comment," *American Indian Magazine,* 6, no. 4 (Winter 1919): 161–2.

may be difficult and the exposures of wrongs innumerable, still we believe,—yes, we know, the world is to be made better as a result of these stirring times.

Immortal justice is the vortex around which swing the whirl of human events!

We are seeking to know justice, not as a fable but as a living, active, practical force in all that concerns our welfare!

Actions of the wise leaders assembled in Paris may be guided ostensibly by temporary man-made laws and aims, dividing human interests into domestic and international affairs, but even so those leaders cannot forget the eternal fact that humanity is essentially one undivided, closely intertwined, fabric through which spiritual truth will shine with increasing brightness until it is fully understood and its requirements fulfilled. The universal cry for freedom from injustice is the voice of a multitude united by afflictions. To appease this human cry the application of democratic principles must be flexible enough to be universal.

Belgium is leading a historic procession of little peoples seeking freedom!

From the very folds of the great allied nations are many classes of men and women clamoring for a hearing. Their fathers, sons, brothers and husbands fought and died for democracy. Each is eager to receive the reward for which supreme sacrifice was made. Surely will the blood-soaked fields of No-Man's Land unceasingly cry out until the high principles for which blood spilled itself, are established in the governments of men.

Thus in vast procession to Paris, we recognize and read their flying banners.

Labor organizations are seeking representation at the Peace Conference. Women of the world, mothers of the human race, are pressing forward for recognition. The Japanese are taking up the perplexing problem of race discrimination.

The Black man of America is offering his urgent petition for representation at the Conference; and already President Wilson has taken some action in his behalf by sending to Paris, Dr. Moton, of Tuskeegee Institute accompanied by Dr. Du Bois.

A large New York assembly of American men and women wirelessed, it is reported, to President Wilson while he was in mid-ocean, enroute to Paris, requesting his aid in behalf of self-government for the Irish people.

The Red man asks for a very simple thing—citizenship in the land that was once his own,—America. Who shall represent his cause at the World's Peace Conference? The American Indian, too, made the supreme sacrifice for liberty's sake. He loves democratic ideals. What shall world democracy mean to his race?

There never was a time more opportune than now for America to enfranchise the Red man!

Charles Eastman Sees the End of War as the Moment to End the "Petty Autocracy" of the Indian Office
1919

Like Zitkala Ša, Charles Eastman believed that the end of the war and the excitement generated by Woodrow Wilson's soaring rhetoric provided an opportunity for American Indian political leaders to advance the group's agenda. Reminding the public that Indians had contributed heavily to the war effort, he suggested a way in which Native Americans could share in the nation's victory. A universal grant of citizenship, he argued, would reduce the power of the Indian Office and help Indian people to become less "dependent and beggarly." Like most members of the Society of American Indians, Eastman had the vague sense that with citizenship would come political power and greater economic self-sufficiency. Hampered by Indian Office regulations, and well aware of the government's willingness to surrender tribal resources to outside interests, he and his colleagues saw little value in continued federal guardianship. The first problem before him appeared to be the Indian community's lack of political power; citizenship would remedy that. Posing an argument not unlike the one suffragists had recently used, Eastman also suggested that Indian voters would bring a new spiritual element to civilized life and that their participation in politics would soften and humanize the public arena.

Charles A. Eastman, "The Indian's Plea for Freedom," *American Indian Magazine*, 6, no. 4 (Winter 1919): 162–5.

I believe this to be an opportune moment for the "little peoples" of the earth to plead for a better observance of their individuality and rights by the more powerful and ruling nations. For we must admit that every race, however untutored, has its ideals, its standards of right and wrong, which are sometimes nearer the Christ principle than the common standards of civilization.

Certainly under the leadership of Woodrow Wilson, we of the United States have an opportunity splendid and far reaching, which may never come again. If the coming Peace Congress will deliberate unselfishly in the interests of humanity, if we can eliminate purely national bias and suspicion, then the world's after-council must establish a new international relationship. And this new order must begin at home. The old rule, the old ambitions for world domination by discovery and conquest must forever pass.

The world is tired, sick, and exhausted by a war which has brought home to us the realization that our boasted progress is after all mainly industrial and commercial—a powerful force, to be sure, but being so unspiritual, not likely to be lasting or stable. On the other hand, being so powerful it might have been expected to be destructive and therefore cruel. The intellectual development connected with it has been largely heartless and soulless. The education of the child has subordinated his higher instincts to the necessities of business. Christ has been preached in vain, since his most unmistakable and unequivocal declarations are directly opposed to our excess of material development, social injustice and the accumulation of wealth.

Now we have come to a point when we may at least hope that this tremendous machine will be used toward a better readjustment of human relationships. An Indian must admire our President for the stand he has taken. It seems we are in a position to pilot the bark of humanity into a safe harbor, if this high stand can be sustained by the allies.

When the vexed Irish question and other knotty problems come up at the peace table, we may be reminded that we too, here in America, have our race troubles. How can our nation pose as the champion of the "little peoples" until it has been fair to its own? "We, too, demand our freedom!" cry those modern Greeks, the North American Indians. Their request is not hard to grant, since it involves no separate government or territory. All we ask is full citizenship. Why not? We offered our services and our money in this war, and more in proportion to our number and means than any other race or class of the population. Yet there are people who insist on keeping us the "wards of the Government," apparently for no other reason than to use our money and our property for their own benefit. . . .

The Indian Bureau, instead of being the servant of the people and of the Indians in accordance with treaty stipulations, has grown into a petty autocracy. The whole system reminds me of the story of Two-Face in the Sioux legend. He stole a child to feed on his tender substance, sucking his blood while still living, and if any one protested, or aroused by the baby's screams, attempted a rescue, he would pat it tenderly and pretend to caress it. This fine intention of the people to develop the Indian into useful citizens has given rise to an institution which is doing them positive injury. . . .

In view of all that the world has just suffered in the name of justice and a fair deal for all, we appeal to all fair-minded Americans. Is it not our due that we should call this fair land ours with you in full brotherhood? Have we not defended bravely its liberties and may we not share them? We do not ask for territorial grant or separate government. We ask only to enjoy with Europe's sons the full privileges of American citizenship.

Robert Yellowtail Calls for Self-Determination
1919

Young enough to have been Zitkala Ša's student at Carlisle or a youthful patient of either Charles Eastman or Carlos Montezuma, Robert Yellowtail (1889?–1988) represented the rising generation of Indian leaders. While educated at boarding schools like their predecessors, members of this new group were more likely to have come to prominence amid the political competition in reservation communities than to have been adopted by missionaries or educated at eastern universities. Unlike Eastman, Bonnin, Montezuma, and Parker, they came of age struggling with other educated young men and women for a voice in community affairs. This struggle carried them through the variety of organizations—tribal business councils, groups advocating various tribal claims, YMCA

"Address by Robert Yellowtail in Defense of the Rights of the Crow Indians, and the Indians Generally, Before the Senate Committee on Indian Affairs, September 9, 1919." *U.S. Senate Report 219,* 66th Cong., 1st sess., serial 7590 (Washington, D.C.: Government Printing Office, 1919).

**Figure 12.
Robert Yellowtail.**
This photograph of
Robert Yellowtail
was probably taken
shortly after he left
Sherman Institute,
a government
boarding school in
Riverside, Califor-
nia. During several
years at Sherman,
Yellowtail had
become fascinated
with American law
and had worked
diligently to polish
his rhetorical skills.
By 1907, Yellowtail
would become a
leading defender of
tribal interests.
Courtesy Little Big
Horn College
Archives.

*groups, and intertribal assemblies — that characterized reservation life
in the first decades of the twentieth century. As new issues arose during
those years, leadership structures headed by traditional chiefs often
declined in influence. Should reservation resources be leased to outside
interests? If so, to whom should the lessee report? Who should grant
rights of way through reservation territories? Who should oversee tribal
policemen and the tribal courts? Who should represent the tribe when it
dealt with federal authorities?*

*A member of the Crow tribe of Montana, Robert Yellowtail attended
the local agency school before being sent to the Sherman Institute in
Riverside, California, for high school. Yellowtail completed his formal
schooling at Sherman and remained in southern California for three
years studying law in the office of a local attorney. He returned to Montana in 1910 and began raising cattle on his allotment in the Little Big*

Horn valley, not far from Sheridan, Wyoming. But the young and bookish Yellowtail was not content to be a rancher. His interest in the law and his concern for tribal affairs quickly drew him into local politics. He served on the tribe's first business committee and was an outspoken member at local assemblies called to oppose the opening of unallotted tribal lands to non-Indian homesteaders. That effort—led by local white politicians—focused on securing passage of a congressional act that would unilaterally reduce the boundaries of the Crow reservation. Strenuous campaigns by tribal leaders blocked this proposal in Congress for more than a decade, but by 1919 it appeared that the tribe's enemies would finally be successful. Yellowtail led a delegation to Washington, D.C., that attempted to negotiate a compromise bill. Their efforts produced the Crow Act, approved by Congress in April 1920.

The following excerpts are taken from a lengthy speech Yellowtail delivered extemporaneously before the Senate Committee on Indian Affairs in defense of the Crow reservation's existing borders. This remarkable address incorporates much of the language Woodrow Wilson had been using both in Paris and in his defense of the League of Nations. Yellowtail's speech was delivered while President Wilson was engaged in his nationwide speaking tour on behalf of the league—and only days before the president's collapse in Pueblo, Colorado, which brought that struggle to an end. The Crow leader's words demonstrate how deeply the war effort had affected tribal leaders and foreshadow the defenses of Indian self-determination that congressional committees would hear in the decades to come.

Mr. Chairman and gentlemen of the committee, the American Indian, also a creature of God, claims, as you yourselves do, to be endowed with certain inalienable rights, among which are life, liberty, and the pursuit of happiness. He further maintains as his inherent right the right to choose the manner in which he shall seek his own happiness. . . .

[Yellowtail then reviewed the history of treaty making between the United States government and the Crow tribe, emphasizing the "covenants" the two groups had forged.]

Now, then, Mr. Chairman, if you look through these sacred covenants you will not find in any of them any reservations or prior agreements to take or sell any portion of our lands so set aside against our wishes for schools or any other purposes to any State or to anybody else, but, on the other hand, it was solemnly agreed that no portion of it shall be disposed of until our consent thereto had been duly given. This was the condition of our agreement then.

Mr. Chairman, the fact of the matter has been that from the day that we treated with your commissioners for presumably a new birth of freedom equal to at least the one which we gave up at your bidding, and in many respects you assured us that it would be better, and taking you at your word and right then and there turning right about face, we followed you as a child follows its father, believing, because of your presence and the faith we reposed in you, that there would be no cause for any alarm, we followed you into what was then a perfect dark. Mr. Chairman, how well you have performed your side of this covenant and how well you have fulfilled this trust that we unhesitatingly reposed in you we leave to the world at large to judge.

Mr. Chairman, it is peculiar and strange to me, however, that after such elaborate and distinct understandings it should develop that today, after over half a century since our agreement, you have not upon your statute books nor in your archives of law, so far as I know, one law that permits us to think free, act free, expand free, and to decide free without first having to go and ask a total stranger that you call the Secretary of the Interior, in all humbleness and humiliation, "How about this, Mr. Secretary, can I have permission to do this"? and "Can I have permission to do that"? etc. Ah, Mr. Chairman, if you had given us an inkling then of what has since transpired, I am sure that our fathers would have then held their ground until every last one of them were dead or until you saw fit to guarantee to us in more explicit assurances something more humane, something more of that blessing of civil life, peculiar to this country alone that you call "Americanism."

Mr. Chairman, your President but yesterday assured the people of this great country, and also the people of the whole world, that the right of self-determination shall not be denied to any people, no matter where they live, nor how small or weak they may be, nor what their previous conditions of servitude may have been. He has stood before the whole world for the past three years at least as the champion of the rights of humanity and the cause of the weak and dependent peoples of this earth. He has told us that this so-called league of nations was conceived for the express purpose of lifting from the shoulders of burdened humanity this unnecessary load of care. If that be the case, Mr. Chairman, I shall deem it my most immediate duty to see that every Indian in the United States shall do what he can for the speedy passage of that measure, but, on the other hand, Mr. Chairman, this thought has often occurred to me, that perhaps the case of the North American Indian may never have entered the mind of our great President when he uttered those solemn words; that, perhaps, in the final draft of this league of nations document a proviso might be inserted to read something like this: "That in no case shall this be construed to mean that the Indians of the United States shall be entitled to the rights and privileges expressed herein, or the right of self-determination, as it is understood herein, but that their freedom and future shall be left subject to such rules and regulations as the Secretary of the Interior may, in his discretion, prescribe." I and the rest of my people sincerely hope and pray that the President, in his great scheme of enforcing upon all the nations of the earth the adoption of this great principle of the brotherhood of man and nations, and that the inherent right of each one is that of the right of self-determination, I hope, Mr. Chairman, that he will not forget that within the boundaries of his own nation are the American Indians, who have no rights whatsoever—not even the right to think for themselves. . . .

Mr. Chairman, I hold that the Crow Indian Reservation is a separate semisovereign nation in itself, not belonging to any State, nor confined within the boundary lines of any State of the Union, and that until such proper cessions, as has been agreed to and as expressed in our covenant, have been duly complied with no Senator, or anybody else, so far as that is concerned, has any right to claim the right to tear us asunder by the continued introduction of bills here without our consent and simply because of our geographical proximity to his State or his home, or because his constituents prevail upon him so to act; neither has he the right to dictate to us what we shall hold as our final homesteads in this our last stand against the ever-encroaching hand, nor continue to disturb our peace of mind by a constant agitation to deprive us of our lands, that were, to begin with, ours, not his, and not given to us by anybody. This nation should be only too ready, as an atonement for our treatment in the past, to willingly grant to the Indian people of this country their unquestionable and undeniable right to determine how much of their own lands they shall retain as their homes and how much they shall dispose of to outsiders. . . .

[Yellowtail then went on to argue in favor of allowing Indians to bring cases before the U.S. Court of Claims without having to secure congressional permission or to seek Indian Office approval for their attorneys,

and to call for a blanket extension of American citizenship to all Native Americans.]

Now, in conclusion, Mr. Chairman, permit me to say that the Indians of this country will grow better and become better and more intelligent and useful citizens, just in proportion as you make it possible for them to be freer and happier; just in proportion as you permit fewer thrusts and snatches at their lands; just in proportion as you allow them to exercise more intellectual liberty; just in proportion as you permit them personal liberty, free thought, and the freest expression thereof, for free thought never gave us anything else but the truth; just exactly the same as your own race has grown better, just in proportion to their exercise of freedom of body, and mind, and thought, plus the freest expression thereof; the history of all nations tell us that they have grown only better just in proportion as they have grown free, and I am here, gentlemen, to advocate that proposition for the American Indian, who still is held in bondage as a political slave; by this great Government as intellectual slaves, and as intellectual serfs; and now, gentlemen, I ask of you, that has not the time arrived when we ought to begin at least to think of giving to these people more of the essence of that happier life as you live it, and to permit them to enjoy a little more of that enviable condition of freedom peculiar only to American civil life that you call "Americanism"? . . .

7

After the War:
Reservation Indians Speak Out

Indians' participation in World War I, and the expanding pace of allotment and leasing led federal officials in the postwar era to believe that the campaign to assimilate Indians into the American mainstream was nearing completion. Congressmen and Indian Office officials predicted that Native American farmers and laborers would soon be indistinguishable from their white neighbors. With American Indians fighting alongside American troops in Europe, American Indian lands being plowed up for crops in the West, and American Indian communities being divided into individual homesteads, it seemed obvious that the long-predicted day when Indians would "vanish" was within reach.

Ironically, the events white people viewed as evidence of Indian assimilation frequently carried an exact opposite meaning for Native Americans. Having served in the war, Indians felt that they deserved respect for their sacrifice. The widespread leasing of reservation lands that took place in order to boost wartime food production was not a source of pride for people who saw outside contractors profiting from their resources. The division of tribal lands worried Indian parents who wondered how their children would survive without any land of their own or a share in the tribal estate. Indian people expressed their pride in the American victory in the war, but it was more often pride in their community's achievements rather than in a national triumph. Although willing to serve the Stars and Stripes, many Natives did not believe that their war efforts had eliminated the cultural and economic barriers separating them from the American majority.

In the immediate postwar years, a series of congressional hearings took place in Washington and on reservations across the country that were intended to improve the efficiency of the Indian Office's operations and to hasten the final division and dismemberment of Indian communities. The first of these, a general investigation conducted by the House Committee on Indian Affairs, occurred between October 1919 and June 1920. In the space of nine months, the Republican committee chair, Homer Snyder of New York, and eight colleagues traveled nine thousand miles and questioned nearly two hundred witnesses. Later sessions organized by Snyder and his Senate counterparts gave dozens of American Indian leaders an opportunity to air complaints and respond to government initiatives.

The government officials' agenda throughout this process was clear—to grant Indians citizenship, to complete allotment, and, in the words of Snyder's 1920 panel, to set Native Americans on a path to "work out their own salvation." The attitude was reflected in one agent's insistence that "as soon as the nation rids itself of dependents," the more virile it can become."[1] But what Snyder and his colleagues heard often revealed that the reality of everyday Indian life did not square with the government's rosy declarations. They found many tribes descending into poverty and many agency branches where Indian Office facilities and support staff were inadequate. The relatively simple scenario that underlay the allotment program—individuals transformed by their ownership of individual homesteads into replicas of white Americans—had not been fulfilled. They heard from individuals who had lost their land to real estate speculators, as well as others who could not farm because they could not obtain cash for seed and machinery or who could not transport their crops from their isolated homesteads to the nation's commodity markets.

It was even more disturbing, however, for legislators to hear from the Indians who testified that they had little interest in becoming a part of Anglo-American culture. Absorbed in local issues, these people continued to inhabit a world bounded by their Indian identity and their social class. Not only did the speakers at these hearings appear isolated from the American economy, but they seemed to inhabit a social world that rarely overlapped with that of their white neighbors. The testimony of Native leaders marked a deepening of the antagonism between advocates of "civilization" and Native Americans.

Educated Indians who had come of age at the beginning of the Progressive Era had spent the previous generation calling on the American majority to recognize their group's claims. They had criticized government policy, unmasked the white majority's hypocrisy, and

[1] See U.S. Congress, House, *Indians of the United States, Field Investigation,* 66 Congress, 3 Session, House Report 1133, pp. 1–18; Frederick E. Hoxie, *A Final Promise: The Campaign to Assimilate the Indians, 1880–1920* (Lincoln: University of Nebraska Press, 1984), 182.

demanded recognition as a distinct community that deserved more than a small corner of their tribal homeland and pious sermons from government-sponsored missionaries. In effect, these Native American intellectuals and national leaders had warned all who might hear them that they did not believe themselves to be on the verge of extinction or transformation into red versions of white people. The testimony legislators heard during the early 1920s confirmed those warnings. When they took the witness stand before these congressional committees, tribal leaders were not simply talking back to the government; they were articulating issues and framing concerns that would preoccupy their communities for decades to come. Indian leadership was passing to a new generation that was building its case on the foundations laid by their outspoken predecessors in the Progressive Era.

Ojibwe Leaders Protest Government Proposals to Abolish Their Reservation
1920

The Indian Office established the White Earth Reservation in northwestern Minnesota in 1867. Located on the edge of the Red River prairie, the reservation contained farming lands government agents had hoped Ojibwe settlers would use to establish individual homesteads as the first step in their assimilation into the American mainstream. Between 1867 and the end of the century, Ojibwe families from across the state moved to White Earth to take up allotments and to enroll their children in government schools. By 1900 more than 4,000 allotments had been made. On paper at least, White Earth was a model reservation that demonstrated the wisdom of the allotment policy.

But while the White Earth Reservation transported individuals to homesteads and schools, it did not solve the problems of Indian poverty. Many tribal members resisted the government's insistence that they take up farming, preferring instead to settle among the lakes and pine groves along the reservation's eastern border. There they tried to subsist on game

---

Testimony of Louis Aynesnassung and George Walters, "Chippewas of Minnesota," Hearings Before the House Committee on Indian Affairs, 66 Congress, 2 Session, January 21 to March 22, 1920.

and occasional wage labor. Ojibwe families that selected allotments in agricultural areas faced problems familiar to other small farmers at the time: uncertain prices, pressure to acquire expensive machinery, and high transportation costs. Indian farmers also faced stiff competition from white settlers who, unlike Native Americans, could qualify for bank loans and agitate for railroad regulation. Despite the "progress" of allotment, then, Ojibwe wealth declined during the first decades of the new century. Even the most industrious tribal members predicted that the future would offer little more than grinding poverty.

In addition to economic hardship, Ojibwe residents of White Earth faced divisions within their own ranks. Among the bands that migrated to the new reservation in the late nineteenth century had been groups of traders and small farmers, most of mixed European and Native American ancestry, who had settled on agricultural allotments and cooperated with government and business interests. When it came to reservation affairs, the entrepreneurial "mixed-bloods" generally favored allotment and the pro rata division of both tribal resources and the income from timber sales and other government payments. Within the tribe they became the party of individualism and business development, while their opponents, who called themselves "full-bloods," favored continuing communal land ownership and separation from whites.

In the first decades of the twentieth century the two groups battled for control of White Earth's future. The mixed-bloods favored dropping the remaining restrictions on the sale of individual allotments and distributing all remaining tribal assets to the membership. Full-bloods countered by challenging many individuals' right to be enrolled as tribal members and insisting that the government recognize the authority of the traditional — and unelected — chiefs. The latter issue became particularly important as the shifting composition of the tribal population placed mixed-bloods in the majority. As their numbers dwindled, full-blood leaders came to refer to themselves as "real Indians" and to their opponents as frauds.

The contest between White Earth assimilationists and their opponents reached a climax in 1913, when a group of mixed-blood leaders from several Ojibwe reservations gathered to form the General Council of the Chippewa. The goal was to strengthen the tribe's hand in dealing with the government by uniting under a single banner, but their full-blood opponents condemned the innovation as a dangerous power grab that would dispossess traditional leaders once and for all. By 1917 the council had proposed that Congress liquidate the tribe's property and transfer all government schools to state control. The traditionalists battled back, but they could not match the assimilationists' numbers; in 1919 they

Figure 13.   An Anishinaabe Family.

This portrait of an Ojibwe family, taken in 1905, reflects the mixed heritage that so confused the legislators and government officials who looked for "solutions" to the tribe's problems. All of the family members wear cotton clothing—shirts, dresses, trousers—but still display the beaded sashes and leggings that mark the distinctive tribal heritage. Similarly, Ojibwe leaders promised loyalty to the United States but insisted on following their own leaders and developing their own approach to modern American life.

Minnesota Historical Society.

decided to withdraw from the General Council in order to avoid having their position defeated by the mixed-blood majority.

The first document in this chapter contains the testimony of two Ojibwe traditionalists speaking in opposition to the General Council's proposal to dispose of the tribe's assets. Appearing before the House Committee on Indian Affairs, Louis Aynesnassung, an elder from the Fon du Lac reserve near Lake Superior, and George Walters (also called Kahgondaush), from White Earth, challenged both the substance of the proposed legislation and the credentials of their opponents. They bitterly opposed the idea of liquidating the tribe's property and claimed that their opponents were acting without community support. It is also significant that the speakers indicated that they would prefer to base their relationship with federal authorities on the Treaty of 1842, the agreement that recognized the territory controlled by each of the Ojibwe bands as well as the authority of traditional tribal chiefs.

Aynesnassung and Walters demonstrated that the assimilation process was deeply complicated and entirely unpredictable. Given the cultural loyalties of these two men, it would be difficult to have faith in the allotment process. Their testimony made clear that groups of Indian people continued to place their first allegiance with their tribes, claiming that those who followed the government's prescribed path were not "real Indians."

Statement of Louis Aynesnassung (Interpreted by John Goslin) and George Walters (Interpreted by William Lufkins)

Mr. Elston:[1] Whom do you represent?

Mr. Aynesnassung: I represent the various tribes in the State of Minnesota; the balance are those from Wisconsin.

Mr. Elston: What are the names of the tribes?

Mr. Aynesnassung: The Chippewa Tribe of Minnesota and Wisconsin.

Mr. Elston: Are you chief or elected representative of those Indians?

Mr. Aynesnassung: Yes.

Mr. Elston: Of what band?

Mr. Aynesnassung: Fond du Lac Reservation, Minn.

Mr. Elston: State what you want the committee to know and what objection, if any, you have to this bill. . . .

Mr. Aynesnassung: The delegation you see here present at this meeting are members of the Chippewa Tribe, representing the various

---

[1]*John A. Elston* (1874–1921), Republican congressman from California.

bands of Indians on the reservations from Minnesota and Wisconsin. I came here with the purpose to look into the interests of the treaty right which we have in common, the treaty that was made in 1842. That was my purpose when I left where I came from, but since this bill has been brought before us I will speak in behalf of the Chippewa Tribe. That is, the delegates from this part of the country do not know any such bill is being proposed by any delegates that are supposed to represent the Chippewa Tribe. We have not heard what the bill was for until we arrived here.

Mr. Elston: Are you for or against the bill?

Mr. Aynesnassung: Any bill or any legislation which concerns my tribe where I come from and that I do not know anything about, I oppose it; but if I should happen to be told and consulted about it, well, I will think and consider and do what is right. . . .

Mr. Elston: Have you read the bill or had it read to you?

Mr. Aynesnassung: Yes; it was read to me and I have it here.

Mr. Elston: What points in the bill or what parts of the bill are objectionable?

Mr. Aynesnassung: The bill that I have aloft in my hand here is a bill that I do not understand and have not been consulted or given an explanation thereof, and I oppose it for this reason, that any such bill is the custom amongst the tribes wherever such a bill is proposed to be passed that is requested that the Government officials consult with the Indians, as I understand, and, therefore, I believe that when such a bill is being proposed, before it becomes legislation, I should be consulted as to what opinion I may have, as it may help me to a certain extent, if explained in a proper manner, and it comes on the basis of a legal principle. I do oppose it for this reason, that the delegates that are supposed to represent my tribes where I come from are not legally appointed by the Chippewa Tribe of Indians. They are not appointed by a legal council. It does not come from the right source, and I have not been notified by these delegates that were sent here to propose this bill. . . .

Mr. Elston: Do you expect to be competent or do your people expect to be competent before long, and when they reach their competency will they have the same rights with the others?[2]

---

[2]The allotment laws provided that once an individual was judged "competent," he or she would obtain a fee-simple title to their land and their land would become taxable by local authorities. While government officials saw competency as a goal—hence Elston's question—Native leaders quickly learned that obtaining that status increased the possibility that a person would lose his land. It is therefore not surprising that Mr. Aynesnassung does not reply directly to Mr. Elston's question.

Mr. Aynesnassung: I understand the meaning and purpose of this bill, but I say here that it is the right of my people. We do not know the persons that drew up this bill. We do not know their character. We do not know them personally and we do not know them to refer them, do not know their history or their principle, and if I want such a man I want somebody that I know to represent me and do an act that would benefit me. There has been an appropriation made here for all these delegates that have come here from time to time, to defray their expenses and all such as that, but of the appropriation that has been granted to them for their expenses, the remainder of it after the expenses have been defrayed, they have divided among the few that have been here at Washington. That is what we object to, and I say that if I wanted that man to represent me, I would have the council of mine appoint a delegate that should represent me. But I do not know this gentleman or any of the gentlemen that presented this bill and, therefore, I protest against it. . . .

Mr. Elston: He said that they had no notification of this delegation coming on here; that is, this other delegation [the General Council of the Chippewa]. How is that? Was it not made public there in that country and did not most people know that that delegation was coming on here?

Mr. Aynesnassung: They had a council where they did not notify Indians what his purpose was. In my council I have a council hall where I hold councils and there it is my desire when any tribal matter comes up for discussion that it is the proper place to bring this matter up and tell me what the object of it is, and then I would be satisfied. But where I simply hear that they will only want a certain type of Indians to meet at a certain place, that is where an Indian is barred out again. . . .

Mr. Elston: Are you the chief of your tribe by inheritance or election?

Mr. Aynesnassung: It comes from away back, my grandfather and great-grandfather have been chief, and my father was chief, and now I am the chief.

Mr. Elston: Have you any specific objections to the bill? . . .

Mr. Aynesnassung: If I proposed any such bill to be passed, I would only ask the gentleman to have legislation passed that would not conflict with any of our Indian property [rights]. . . .

Mr. Goslin: He means to say that the Fond du Lac Indians have no authority or power or any title on the White Earth Reservation, and the White Earth Reservation has no power to rule or control the tribes of the Red Lake Reservation.

Mr. Elston: Are you satisfied to let things stay as they are now without any legislation?

Mr. Aynesnassung: Delegates who are here at present were sent here for the purpose of discussing the 1842 treaty for certain rights that they have in the treaty and after their affairs have been settled properly and gotten what their purpose is in coming here, what they were sent here for, they will go back to their people and hold a general council of the tribes included in the treaties, and then they propose to make a new treaty which will settle the standing of their people. . . .

Mr. Elston: What proportion of all the bands or of the total population in all the reservations does this delegation represent? Is it a half or a third or a fourth, or what is the percentage of the total Indian population which this delegation represents?

Mr. Aynesnassung: I can not figure out the percentage that I represent. I can furnish you a list of names that I represent here. . . .

Mr. Elston: You think it is only about one-fifth of the whole Indian population that this delegation represents? . . .

Mr. Goslin: They represent about 75 per cent of the tribe where they come from. The property owners among the Indians are so varied that the agitators are only about 25 per cent of them.

Mr. Carss:[3] Were these men present when you held the council at White Earth last fall and selected delegates to come down here?

Mr. Aynesnassung: The gentleman standing over there [Mr. Arten], I did not know that he was coming to Washington at all until I saw it in the paper that I get at home. I did not know who elected him to represent the tribe.

Mr. Carss: Then you were not present at that meeting where these delegates were chosen?

Mr. Aynesnassung: The council that compose the Chippewa Tribe, I always hear of such a council going to be held, but the half-breeds, I never heard of their council. . . . I was advised by the people I represent here when I left where I come from not to mingle with any other people or any other parties or other delegates that may be here, but since I got here and saw this bill I notified the people right away what was going on and they told me not to do anything except what they sent me for. My purpose is to look after the treaty of 1842.

---

[3] *William L. Carss* (1865–1931), Farmer-Labor congressman from Minnesota.

Sioux Leaders Protest the Leasing of Tribal Lands
1920

From the outset of the allotment era, it had been clear that some individuals would not be able to farm their land. The elderly, orphans, and people who were otherwise unable to farm found themselves owners of homesteads they could not develop. When first passed, the Dawes Severalty Act did not allow allottees to lease their holdings, but in 1891 an amendment was enacted that allowed agents to lease the property of those who, because of "age or disability," could not cultivate the soil. A few years later "inability" was added as a reason to allow leasing, but relatively few individuals used the provision to rent their allotments. After the turn of the century, however, the expansion of allotment and the consequent dwindling of areas available for large-scale farming increased the pressure on the Indian Office to liberalize its leasing policy. The number of approved leases rose steadily.

World War I dramatically increased the pressure to lease allotments and other tribal lands, both because it created a vast market for American foodstuffs and because it introduced "patriotism" into the discussion of how best to manage the Indian estate. Woodrow Wilson's commissioner of Indian affairs, Texan Cato Sells, responded eagerly to the renewed call, arguing that all resources on Indian lands should be made available for the war effort. By 1920 more than 4 million acres of tribal and allotted land were under lease.

Among the reservations most dramatically affected by the new leasing initiative were the large Lakota Sioux reservations in western South Dakota. At Pine Ridge, home to the Oglala bands that had followed Red Cloud and Crazy Horse in the nineteenth century, hundreds of thousands of acres of range land were leased to stockmen. By 1919 three-quarters of the reservation was leased to serve as pastures for cattle and sheep. "For the first time . . . in the history of the reservation," the Pine Ridge superintendent wrote, "all of the grass is being utilized in the production of beef and mutton, bringing a revenue to the Indians never

[1]U.S. Bureau of Indian Affairs, Superintendent's Annual Narrative and Statistical Report, from Field Jurisdictions" (Washington, D.C., National Archives Microfilm 1011, 1975), Pine Ridge, 1919, 2.

Testimony of Joseph Horn Cloud and James H. Red Cloud, "Complaints of the Pine Ridge Sioux," Hearings Before the Committee on Indian Affairs," House of Representatives, 66 Congress, 2 Session, April 6, 1920

Figure 14.   James Red Cloud.
Following the death of the nineteenth-century war leader Red
Cloud in 1909, a younger generation of Lakota men stepped forward to assert their leadership within the Pine Ridge and Rose-
bud Reservation communities. James Red Cloud, one of the
original Red Cloud's grandsons, was one such newcomer. While
too young to have won traditional war honors in the fighting
against the Americans, James Red Cloud considered himself
responsible for the welfare of the families who had cast their lot
with his grandfather thirty years before.
Courtesy of the Edward E. Ayer Collection, The Newberry Library,
Chicago.

heretofore obtained by them." [1] *Government officials clearly expected Native Americans to welcome the new program and the increased income it produced.*

When Congressman Snyder's committee heard from the Indians of Pine Ridge in April of 1920, they discovered the Lakotas were not pleased with the leasing program. Facing the committee were a young political leader named Joseph Horn Cloud and James Red Cloud, grandson of the famous chief. These two leaders had a broader view of the leasing enterprise than the agency superintendent or the commissioner of Indian affairs had expected. They were not pleased, for example, to have their own ranching activities disrupted by the new herds that had "overrun" their homeland. They resented the fact that income from the leases went to the superintendent to support agency activities and schools rather than to individual landowners or the tribal council. It seemed to the two Natives that the Indian Office was treating their range land as part of the public domain. As Horn Cloud declared, local officials ignored their complaints, preferring to "sit there smoking their cigars and writing reports."

These statements reveal that the people at Pine Ridge viewed their lands differently than did government officials and western ranchers. The reservation was something more than an economic commodity to be "developed," and the community living there was concerned with more— despite its poverty—than maximizing its income. The residents' concern for the survival of their less-productive but locally managed stock operation, and their demand that local officials respect their concerns, indicated an attachment to their land and their tribe that had not been eradicated by allotment. By the end of the session, Congressman Snyder ["The Chairman" in the following transcript] was forced to reiterate the government's rationale for governing Indian communities unilaterally and without consulting their leaders. A hearing on leasing became a discussion of what the witnesses' grandchildren would call sovereignty.

Statement of Joseph Horn Cloud and James H. Red Cloud

Mr. Horn Cloud: I want to say a few words, and I want you to consider them closely for me. We have had a lot of trouble on our reservation, and we can not bear it any longer. That is the only reason why we come over here. One difficulty is because this bad leasing business came in, and we are badly off. We were better off before that, and we did not have any trouble. Since they began leasing land there, there have been more troubles and more disputes over land, and that is what is causing all the trouble. It is the trouble with these young men who are able-bodied and had been getting along all right up until the times these leases were made. Now, they are overrun by stockmen, and they have trouble in raising their own stock. Other troubles have arisen from the leases. From the way it is now, if an Indian's stock gets in among the white man's cattle or horses they get lost. It is like losing an ant in an ant hill. We have had gardens; we have had little gardens and have gotten along fine with them, but since this leasing business we have been damaged. That is one of the reasons. We suffered a whole lot ourselves and our stock have suffered because we can not get any hay lands. The superintendent tells the Indians that even when they refuse to lease their lands they got orders from the Indian Bureau to lease that land whether they want to lease it or not.

There are several cases where I have some leases myself. The moneys that are supposed to be paid for the leases go into the hands of the superintendent, and that is deposited somewhere in some bank. They are supposed to get payment every six months, but when the six months are up they do not get the payments. It goes on for one year or two years before they get payments on the leases. We want to find out whether there is any interest to be paid on this money. We can not get that information from the superintendent. I make the suggestion that the Indians whose money is deposited by the superintendent should have a little notebook or account book or an individual account book so that when we go there we can draw our money out. They could put it down and keep track of what is due them.

The Chairman: Something like a savings-bank book?

Mr. Horn Cloud: Yes, Sir. There are a good many of the Indians who are sick and have money deposited with the superintendent, and they can not get it in time of need. There are a good many of them who have died while waiting for it and trying to get it. I can name a few of them if you want me to.

The Chairman: We want you to.

Mr. Horn Cloud: There was one man by the name of Walking-Under-the-Ground. He had more than $3,000 to his credit, and he could not get any of it. He said that when he was suffering, and in need of clothing and food, he could not get anything, and he died. After he died they wanted to find out who was to get the money. Why did they not give it to the man that owned it in the first place, and not wait until he died and then try to find out who should get the money? He had one son there who is not very well. Furthermore, they went to work and buried that old man with rough lumber. There was another called Shoulder; and there is another one named Running-Jumper. Running-Jumper had money to his credit with the superintendent, and his daughter also had some, and they tried to get some of it, but could not. Then the daughter went to work and sold a mare and colt in order to get a coffin for her father. This daughter of his had something like $600 of her own to her credit. They [the family] asked him [the Superintendent] if there would be clothes for this dead man, and they said, "Why not give it to him when he was alive?" We know, or we remember, how other superintendents were that had been on our reservation, and this superintendent we have now is different from any of them we have ever had. We know a good many men who respect us and who greet us whenever we meet them.

We go to this superintendent's office to have a talk with him, and he tells us to get out; that he does not have time to talk to us. He wants to talk to white men there. I would like to ask you one question, and that is this, whether that office is there for the Indians, or for the white men? I would like to know what you expect us to do with our complaints that we make when we go up there. We are the original owners of this land, and we are having the most suffering. What we want is to remove that superintendent, and if he is not removed, we know that there will be some trouble that will arise over it. Then, who will be to blame? We have been sent here by the tribe to bring these complaints before the Indian Bureau. We never get any satisfaction there, and we come to this committee to have your consideration. We want some men sent out on this reservation so that we can prove our facts. We want them to see these things with their own eyes. . . .

The majority of you have never been on the reservation. That man over there has never been on the reservation and does not know the condition of it, and this man here, Mr. Meritt,[2] just goes by what is reported to him, but aside from that he does not know what is going on. They all do just what you are doing, smoking a cigar.

The Chairman: If we could go to the Pine Ridge Reservation and sit down among the people there, and have a meeting just as we are

---

[2]*Edgar B. Meritt* served as Assistant Commissioner of Indian Affairs in the Wilson, Harding, and Coolidge administrations.

having now, these men would come before the committee and tell us what they are telling us now. Why is not all of the information as available here as if we were hearing it out there? What could you show us out there that you are not showing us here?

Mr. Horn Cloud: I will tell you that they have not been doing right. They sit there smoking their cigars and writing reports. They send them to the bureau, and they approve them. They may want to ask a little increase in order that they may have a little more cigar money. We would like to have this thing investigated.

Mr. Kelly:[3] This man, Mr. Horn Cloud, is a live wire, and I like his dynamic manner. I believe that he is fully able to take care of himself. Now, if the superintendent were taken off the reservation, with all of the Indian Service, and the Indians of the Pine Ridge Reservation were left to take care of themselves and manage their own affairs, could they successfully handle their allotment without any help from the Indian Service at all?

Mr. Horn Cloud: Yes, sir. There are some old men that need a little care, but we could take care of them.

Mr. Kelly: That is what should be done.

Mr. Gandy:[4] For the information of my colleagues on the committee, I will say that it is my recollection that there are approximately 3,000 Indians on the ration roll on the Pine Ridge Reservation.

The Chairman: There is absolutely no use in the Pine Ridge Indians getting any idea that they will be made entirely independent of the Indian Bureau. While you may want to be rid of the Indian Service, it is not within the power of anybody to bring that about now. You could not do it yourself because, as has just been stated, you have 3,000 Indians up there now on the ration roll today. When you gentlemen came in the other day, the first thing you told me was that you wanted to abolish the Indian Bureau, and I told you then that that could not be done. The Indian Bureau will have to exist for many years to come, and your affairs will have to be handled to a greater or lesser degree by the Indian Bureau. The less antagonism you have, the more patient you are, and the more you try to get along with them and not believe they are all bad, the better off you will be. It is not a good thing for a set of men to put themselves up

[3] *M. Clyde Kelly* (1883–1935), Republican congressman from Ohio. Kelly served one term, 1916–18, as a Progressive.

[4] *Henry L. Gandy* (1881–1957), Democratic congressman from South Dakota who served from 1915 to 1921. Gandy was a rancher from Wasta, S.D., near the Pine Ridge reservation.

as being opposed to the people with whom they must deal. We have the same difficulties in practical business life to-day. We have great organizations of labor, and they send their committees to us. We do not always feel like granting their every wish and desire, and it can not always be done, but we must sit down and listen to them. We must talk it over together and try to meet each other on some common ground that will be to the best interest of all parties concerned. It is not a thing for a half dozen men to set themselves up as being opposed to a condition which must exist. . . .

We sometimes nearly come to the conclusion that on the whole it might be a good plan to turn all the Indians loose upon their own resources, but when you come to examine into it and to look into all of its ramifications you must at once conclude it can not be done. I believe that while Mr. Kelly is enthusiastic and patriotic and wants to make the Indians independent of the Indian Service, he himself knows that it can not be done, and that we have got to go on with the system as it is until it can be improved. Now, we are trying to improve the system so that the Indian can get just what he is entitled to until such time as he is able to take his own property and manage it for himself. No one desires more than I do to see the Indians become self-sustaining citizens, and I am working with that end in view, but we must not lose sight of the fact that we have been from 180 to 140 years bringing the Indian to the condition in which he now is. Some people believed that when women were allowed to vote the whole country would be revolutionized and that all the ills of man would be straightened out and corrected immediately.

Now, it seems to me that it is impossible for anybody to believe that something which has been going on for 140 or 150 years, and in which we have developed so many difficulties, could be straightened out by waving a magic wand, or something of that sort. I think I am right when I say to you that we must all work together, and keep out all the antagonism we possibly can. Now I notice that that speech does not get any applause, but when we get through with it, I think you will find that what I have said will come nearer to being what will happen to you than that which Mr. Kelly has said.

[James H. Red Cloud appears]

The Chairman: Whom do you represent?
Mr. Red Cloud: The tribe.

The Chairman: Are you a delegate the same as the previous witness?

Mr. Red Cloud: I am the main delegate, and I take the place of my grandfather, Chief Red Cloud.

The Chairman: You have heard all the previous witness has said?

Mr. Red Cloud: Yes, Sir.

The Chairman: Can you tell us anything different from what the other witness [Joseph Horn Cloud] has said?

Mr. Meritt: Red Cloud is a relative of the famous Chief Red Cloud, one of the best-known Indians in the United States.

Mr. Red Cloud: The first thing I want to say is that I have made an agreement that I would be friends with the Government, in 1914, and we have agreed that if there is any man appointed by the Government I am to help him, whichever way he falls. I, too, fall the same way, and wherever he sheds blood I am to shed blood, and if at any time we need help from each other we are to give it. There are some things going to happen on our reservation and I do not like to see it come on and I don't want any more trouble on our reservation, because there are a good many children among them. The superintendent we have there does not treat the Indians right. When the war was on we leased that land in order to provide for the ones that went across. We wanted that to come to an end when the war was over, and as the war is ended we want that to end, too. It is pretty hard there for us on the reservation. The reservation is covered with cattle like a whole lot of worms on it. I can not raise any garden and can not do anything. The superintendent went as far as to try to put some Indians in jail for driving cattle away from their gardens. There is a lot of trouble like that on our reservation and that is one of the reasons why we want this lease to be abolished and the superintendent removed and in that way we will get along better.

Winnebago Leaders Ask for Justice

1922

In the early twentieth century, Native American complaints against the United States began to be heard by the U.S. Court of Claims. These hearings were rare at first because federal law stipulated that all suits for damages filed by American Indians had to be approved by Congress prior to being filed. Nevertheless, a few tribes, usually groups with powerful white allies, managed to win approval for their petitions. After World War I, increasing political activity on reservations in general, and the emergence of a group of Washington attorneys who specialized in "Indian law," caused the pace of this process to quicken. Thirty-one claims were submitted to the court before World War I, but in the decade following the war more suits were approved than had been brought in the previous forty years. The Government Accounting Office established a special Tribal Claims Section to prepare financial data related to these suits, and the activities of specialized lawyers and their Indian clients increased.

In January 1922, two Winnebago leaders appeared before the House Committee on Indian Affairs to argue in favor of a bill that would allow their tribe to petition the U.S. Court of Claims. They presented a brief summary of their complaints. The Winnebago had maintained trade and diplomatic relations with the French and the English beginning in the seventeenth century. By the time of the American Revolution they had settled in central Wisconsin and were subsisting by hunting, fishing, farming, and trading furs for tools, cloth, and foodstuffs. They had signed their first treaty of friendship with the United States in 1816. In 1822 the United States had approached the tribe to request the sale of a portion of its Wisconsin territory to the New York Oneida so that the latter group could leave an area where they were being harassed by white settlers and resettle in the Midwest. The Winnebago refused. They did agree to sell land sought by lead miners in 1829 and 1832, but their most dramatic confrontation with the Americans had come in 1837. In that year—five years after the Black Hawk War had taken place in neighboring Illinois and two years after the removal of the Cherokee from Georgia was sealed by the Treaty of New Echota—a group of tribal delegates had been held hostage in Washington, D.C., until they agreed to sell all the Winnebago

---

Testimony of Thomas Big Bear and Whirling Thunder, "Claims of the Winnebago Indians," Hearings Before the Committee on Indian Affairs, House of Representatives, 67 Congress, 2 Session, on H.R. 4571, January 25, 1922.

lands in Wisconsin and move west across the Mississippi. The delegates agreed to the sale only after they were assured by federal officials that the tribe would have eight years to leave Wisconsin. When they returned home, they were informed that the phrase in the treaty they had thought was "eight years" was actually "eight months."

The Winnebago split into two groups in 1837, one group migrating west in conformity with the new treaty and the other remaining illegally in Wisconsin. The "treaty" Winnebago settled first in Iowa before being granted a reservation in Blue Earth, Minnesota. They lived relatively happily at Blue Earth until 1862, when frontier hysteria triggered by the nearby Santee Sioux uprising caused the Indian Office to close the reservation. Some 1,934 Winnebagos were removed by force from Minnesota and transported to Crow Creek, South Dakota, to be resettled. Tragically, only 1,382 tribal members survived the journey. Nearly all of those relocated Winnebago later escaped and made their way to the Missouri River, where they settled among the Omaha. In 1865 the United States created a reservation for the Winnebago in Nebraska.

Those Winnebago who had refused to recognize the 1837 treaty gradually dispersed across ten counties in central Wisconsin. They lived in small family groups, avoiding contact with government officials and hostile whites. The government periodically attempted to round up these resisters, but the victims of their sweeps usually sneaked back to Wisconsin and resumed their previous life. Finally, in 1881, special legislation was approved allowing the Wisconsin Winnebago to file for homesteads and remain exempt from property taxes. By the turn of the century more than 600 such homesteads had been claimed. Unfortunately, the 1881 tax exemption was repealed in 1906, and most of the Wisconsin homesteaders subsequently lost their land.

In the following testimony, Thomas Big Bear and Whirling Thunder, both from the Nebraska Winnebago community, tried to convey some of their tribe's history to the congressional panel. For these leaders, events that had taken place a century earlier were fresh in their minds and were far more important than the Indian Office's allotment and education programs. These men gave their listeners a glimpse of a worldview that did not organize time and progress in the same way as the Indian Office.

Statement of Thomas Big Bear (Interpreted by David Sincere)

The Chairman [Congressman Snyder]: Big Bear may go ahead and state to the committee the facts of the claim of his tribe of Indians. . . .

Mr. Big Bear: I will not take up all of your time, but will tell you from my own knowledge what I know and what I heard from my father and grandfather. The Winnebego Indians are the first ones that met the white people; that is, the Winnebago Indian Tribe claimed to be the first ones that met the white people and made friends with them. When we saw the white men they made friends with us, and I am going to tell the committee the first thing they asked us. I am telling now what I am telling you from my grandfather. At the first council with the white men representing the United States Government they wanted a certain piece of land, wanted to buy a certain piece of land that we owned. The grandfather refused to sell it. Then they wanted a lease and we leased it to them. The commissioner's representative asked Mr. Soldier, Does this land belong to you, or does it belong to the English or the French? And Mr. Soldier, the Indian chief, told them this land belongs to the Indian tribe.

Mr. Jefferis:[5] Was that lease in writing?

Mr. Big Bear: All I can tell you what the Indians did in that transaction is what they said. The department might have taken it down. I do not know, and have never heard, and would not be very sure. The land belonged to the Indians and the English had no claim to this land. Soldier said, "No, this land belongs to me and my tribe and nation." Then this representative of the Government came again and said, "Soldier, I want another piece of land." He pointed to a certain piece of land and said, "I want that land, Soldier, my friend," and Soldier said, "Yes; you can have it." . . .

Mr. Jefferis: About when was it?

Mr. Big Bear: In 1829, after that; that is, the first cession was made in 1829. At that time, when we made the first lease we never realized anything. That was the story I got, but the second time the white man came and wanted another piece of land and when the chief told him he could have it he gave us a few clothes, blankets, etc., and a few traps and a few guns; but never paid us any money, and that is what he owes us and what we want to get from the Government, what it owes us for that.

The Chairman: What you want is pay for the land taken from the tribe at that time?

Mr. Big Bear: When we made the cession the department told us that they were going to take care of the Indians and be friendly to them as long as they live, and that is what we did what they asked us.

[5]*Albert W. Jefferis* (1868–1942), Republican congressman from Omaha, Nebraska.

The Government has been friendly in a way and given us some things, but has never paid what the lands were really worth. . . .

The Chairman: How are the Indians situated today? Have they plenty of land and are they doing well as an Indian tribe?

Mr. Big Bear: We have some land but are not very well off. That is what I am trying to explain to the committee and hope that I will have time so that I can. . . . I am not making any charges against you gentlemen. I am talking about what they did to us these long years ago, about what the Government told us what they would give us: blankets, money, and annuities. But if the representative of the Government would find a few of us in a bunch—the others were out hunting maybe 150 miles away—and they would make their payment and the distribution of their goods and go back and report to the Great Father that they did it all, which they never did. I am making this plea to the Committee here to give us a little information so that we can go after what we think the Government owes us. I am not asking for anything or begging, but only asking for some of our rights. History can tell you that we lived east of here and we wanted our land, but now we are away down west and I want to show you how we have been treated. I am not disputing that the department of the Government gave us something. They did give us something but never what they ought to give us. They gave to some, but the other fellows would be out hunting and if they did not see them they went without it, but only gave to those they saw. . . .

The Chairman: Do you claim that the Government did not give you what the Government agreed to give? . . .

Mr. Big Bear: This is a long story. I am trying to make it short. The Government owed us and owes us now and we want to get what they owe us not only for those pieces of land but other lands since the white man came.

Mr. Leatherwood:[6] Who, if anybody, suggested to you that you come down here now to see about it?

Mr. Big Bear: Down home when they heard about this case the old people got together at a council and they wanted to come here awful bad, but they are old and feeble and could not stand the journey and asked me to come and that is why I am here.

Mr. Jefferis: Are you paying your own expenses, or if not, who is paying your expenses?

Mr. Big Bear: No; I am not paying my own expenses.

---

[6]*Elmer O. Leatherwood* (1872–1929), Republican congressman from Utah.

Mr. Jefferis: Who is paying your expenses?

Mr. Big Bear: The man who is working for me, trying to get money for me, went to the Indian Office and the Indian Office said they did not have any, and Mr. Evans has given me money to come here to present my case.

Mr. Leatherwood: Which Mr. Evans?

Mr. Big Bear: Victor Evans;[7] Mr. Evans down on Ninth Street.

Mr. Leatherwood: Did he give those other Indians money to come down here?

Mr. Big Bear: He did not give them any money, but paid for their transportation, tickets, and hotel bills.

The Chairman: In other words, these attorneys who are working in the interests of these claimants have furnished the money for the representatives of the Winnebago Tribe who are now here to come here and have paid their expenses while here?

Mr. Big Bear: Yes.

Mr. Leatherwood: Do you know how old you are?

Mr. Big Bear: I am 74 years old.

The Chairman: Do you know that when the Winnebagoes ceded the land that they were on the east side of the Mississippi; that they received more than $1,000,000 in money for it? . . .

Mr. Big Bear: All I remember is that at one time there was a big payment, but that the Indians did not get the big payment; the half-breeds, a certain number of half-breeds, got over $1,000 apiece.

The Chairman: The Winnebago Indians at that time ceded this property to the Government for full consideration and moved to some other part of the country. At that time, evidently, the Government must have wound up its obligations to the Winnebagoes. They must have had full pay at that time.

Mr. Big Bear: I can not read. I can not write. Please, brothers, tell me which certain piece of land that you have referred to and I might answer your question?

The Chairman: It was all the land that the Winnebagoes occupied east of the Mississippi River at that time. . . . Is there anything else you wish to tell us?

Mr. Big Bear: This is all I will say, not because that is all the complaint I want to make, but I want to make room for the others to say something. I thank every one of you gentlemen here and you can

[7]*Victor Evans* was an early specialist in American Indian law. He represented several tribes before the Court of Claims.

look at me and see what shape I am in and take consideration of what I have said and pass legislation so that I can get justice before the courts.

Mr. Leatherwood: Why have you never come down here and told about this before?

Mr. Big Bear: The only reason I can give you for that is that my father [came] here twice to see the Great Father and tried to settle with him for land the Government had leased for 30 years. They said "no" we have that money altogether; we are leasing that land and when we get it we will give it to you. He made two demands without any success. Since that [time] my father died and we have never come since then.

Statement of Mr. Whirling Thunder, January 25, 1922 (Interpreted by David Sincere)

The Chairman [Congressman Snyder]: Whom do you represent?

Mr. Whirling Thunder: I represent the Winnebago Indians of Nebraska and Wisconsin. . . . The first thing that I am going to tell the committee is that in Minnesota, we had good homes and we were driven away from there by soldiers.

The Chairman: What year?

Mr. Whirling Thunder: I do not know, but somewhere near the outbreak of the Sioux.

The Chairman: About how long ago was that?

Mr. Whirling Thunder: That was when I was 13 years old.

The Chairman: How old are you now?

Mr. Whirling Thunder: Seventy-two or seventy-three. . . . I was in the house where I lived and soldiers came and told me to get out. I had my little blanket over my shoulders. I got out and they did not allow me to go back and take any more of my personal effects of any kind. They drove us like cattle. We did not have any conveyance of any kind, but they marched us to the city of Mankato.

The Chairman: What had the Indians done, to cause the soldiers to do that?

Mr. Whirling Thunder: I could not tell you the reason they did it. All we were doing there was farming and trying to make a living. That is all I know. They took us to Mankato and put us on a steamboat and we went down the river to St. Paul, on the Mississippi River. They told us they were going to take us; down to Missouri, where the Government was going to give us some land. They never took us down there. They did not take us down to the mouth of the Mississippi. They took us somewhere near St. Joe and locked us in a great tobacco warehouse for two days, locking us in so we could not have a chance to get out as we ought to. That was the treatment we got.

The Chairman: Was this in the Civil War?

Mr. Whirling Thunder: This was before the Civil War that they locked us in that tobacco warehouse, and we had to stay there, and did not have a chance to get out, and had to stay inside. That is the treatment we got.

The Chairman: I think you said it was about the time of the outbreak of the Sioux war in Minnesota?

Mr. Whirling Thunder: The outbreak in Minnesota.

The Chairman: You do not suppose they took the Indians down there for the purpose of keeping them from combining with the Sioux?

Mr. Whirling Thunder: The only reason I can give the committee is that the Winnebagos did not do anything in fighting or helping the Sioux out any; but this land was fertile and the settlers wanted it, and insisted on moving the Indians, and they did move us, and that is the only reason I can give.

The Chairman: Is that about the time you were locked in the tobacco warehouse?

Mr. Whirling Thunder: When they took us across to St. Joe we stayed there a couple of days and a freight train came along, and they put us in box cars. We were all corralled in there and the lock was put on, and we were all put on that freight train. . . . I could not tell you how many they took; half of them first and then they took the other half the next time, and landed them at Crow Creek.

The Chairman: At Crow Creek, where they now reside?

Mr. Whirling Thunder: They are living in Nebraska, now.

The Chairman: They landed them at Crow Creek. How long did they stay at Crow Creek?

Mr. Whirling Thunder: Some of them stayed one year and some of them stayed two years.

The Chairman: Where did they go from there?

Mr. Whirling Thunder: They went to the Omaha Reservation.

The Chairman: How many of them went to the Omaha Reservation?

Mr. Whirling Thunder: At first about 407 came down and the next time more of them came, and the second year all of them came to the Omaha Reservation.

The Chairman: About how many of them were there?

Mr. Whirling Thunder: I can not tell you the number.

The Chairman: Is that where they live now?

Mr. Whirling Thunder: Yes, Sir. . . .

The Chairman: Do you feel that you have personally been injured yourself; and, if so, how much do you think the personal injury is in value?

Mr. Whirling Thunder: I can not tell you. I have no education and have never been to school; but I know I have been mistreated, but I can not tell you the amount in money. . . .

Mr. Jefferis: Did the Winnebagos get part of the Omaha Reservation when they moved in there or not?

Mr. Whirling Thunder: We bought some from the Omahas.

Mr. Jefferis: That is, the Government bought?

Mr. Whirling Thunder: . . . I suppose the Government bought it for us.

The Chairman: In other words, it was probably bought from the money they got from the land that they ceded east of the Mississippi?

Mr. Whirling Thunder: Yes.

The Chairman: Then, you yourself do not know how much the Government owes you either in land or moneys or clothing or anything else?

Mr. Whirling Thunder: That I can not tell you, Mr. Chairman, in figures, because, as I say, I can not read or write; but I know I have been mistreated, because I am old enough and saw it and know it, but I can not tell you figures because I have no education or learning. That is why I came to see you folks. I want an attorney to look after this business.

The Klamath Seek Independence

1924

The final excerpt from the testimony of the early 1920s comes from hearings held before the House Committee on Indian Affairs on a proposal to pay the members of the Klamath tribe an amount equal to the value of their tribal domain. These hearings provided one of the first public discussions of an issue that would engage policymakers for the remainder of

Testimony of Levi Walker and Charles S. Hood, "Klamath Indians of Oregon," Hearings Before a Subcommittee of the Committee on Indian Affairs, House of Representatives, 68 Congress, 1 Session, on H. R. 7351, April 11, 1924.

*the twentieth century: how can Indian people free themselves from fed-
eral supervision? Can communities act as tribes outside the authority of
the Indian Office? These questions would surface in the 1940s and
1950s as white politicians advocated "terminating" federal controls over
tribes, and again in the 1980s and 1990s as tribes sought to place their
relations with Washington, D.C., on a government-to-government basis.
In each of these later periods, the case of the Klamath would provide an
instructive example.*

*A hunting and gathering people whose aboriginal homeland lay in the
plateau region of south-central Oregon, the Klamath were descended
from Klamath, Modoc, and Yahooskin bands who negotiated their title to
a reservation in 1864. By the early twentieth century, the Indian Office
had allotted the Klamath preserve to individual members, but several
hundred thousand acres of rich timber land remained under tribal ownership. The opening of public lands and the gradual sale of Indian allotments to white settlers introduced a large non-Indian population to the
area. By the time of this testimony, non-Native residents of the reservation slightly outnumbered the Klamath.*

*During the 1920s, many Klamath began to protest their continuing
dependency on the Indian Office. Owners of a rich resource, they saw virtually all the income from the tribal forest being used to support the local
Indian Office agency: Klamath funds paid the salaries of federal employees
and teachers, as well as the costs of constructing schools and roads.[1] In
this atmosphere, Klamath leaders began to question why they could not
control these assets themselves.*

*The testimony below concerns a proposal to have the federal govern-
ment loan the members of the Klamath tribe $5 million, the cash equiva-
lent of the value of their tribal forest. The cash would be paid to
individual tribal members; in return, the Klamath forest would be trans-
ferred to the U.S. Forest Service. The speakers are Levi Walker, a prominent member of the Klamath Tribal Council, and Charles S. Hood, a
Carlisle graduate of Modoc ancestry who frequently criticized the Indian
Office. Both men spoke in favor of the plan; they were critical of the government's current policy, but they seemed untroubled that the proposal
might lead to the dissolution of the tribe. The focus of their concern was
the authoritarian nature of federal control over their community. With*

[1]See U.S. Bureau of Indian Affairs, *Superintendent's Annual Narrative and Statistical Reports from Field Jurisdictions* (Washington, D.C. National Archives Microfilm
1011, 1975), Klamath Agency, 1924, 1. It declared in part that the "Klamath Agency
is supported almost entirely from tribal funds derived from the sale of timber on the
reservation."

no cash and no way of using their tribal wealth to finance improvements in their farms and ranches, these Klamath sought a way to remove the restrictions that they believed would bind them in poverty. They spoke for only one side of the debate over the Klamath's future (their opponents were not present at the hearing), but their testimony underscored a dilemma that would become common in the years ahead: federal wardship and dependency versus individual "freedom" and the loss of tribal status.

Although these statements refer to an individual tribal predicament, they underscore the fact that at the end of the Progressive Era, Indians were no more comfortable with the roles assigned them by their civilized supervisors than they were at its start. Concerned about how to act on their choices as Indians, Levi Walker and Charles Hood do not imagine themselves to be backward, dependent, or in need of federal tutelage. Moreover, they are eager to make choices and to participate in the American economy. Their plans carried considerable danger for their community, but they reflect the struggle of Native people to be recognized as fellow Americans, fully capable of shaping their futures, rather than as artifacts of the past who had no alternative than to accept the roles assigned them.

*(*Note: *In 1954 Congress approved a version of this 1924 proposal, and in the process terminated its relationship with the Klamath Tribal Council. The new arrangement proved disastrous for the Klamath, and Congress reversed itself by reestablishing its recognition of the tribe in 1986.)*

Statement of Levi Walker, April 11, 1924

Mr. Walker: . . . We have come to a point where we have to make some change in this business, and I was in hopes the Department of the Interior would lend us assistance in doing it; but instead we have received something that is the reverse.

We have outgrown what you might call "an Indian custom" to a great extent, and in facing that great task, we will have to take the responsibility of citizenship. The laws which governed 40 or 50 years ago should not apply to the Klamath reservation at this day, so it seems to me that, after all, the department should change its policy in handling the Klamath Indians. It should broaden its policy in every respect. The records will show that affairs have come to a point where something must be done, and we have been advised in this city that we can not enact legislation in this Congress to dispose of all the tribal timber. For that reason we have come to the conclusion that $5,000,000 would be the sum that should be distributed among the Klamath Indians, share and share alike. As to noncompetent Indians and as to minor children their money would be handled under the existing law, the same as usual. The only difference would be that money placed to the credit of the Klamath Indians per capita would be in a lump sum at one time, which would enable him to do something for himself, instead of drifting along and finding ourselves away down the river, and worse off than we are now.

Mr. Stalker:[2] In your opinion, how would they use this $4,000 per capita; would they invest it in stock, or in what way would they use it if they had it?

Mr. Walker: Each Indian would have the money invested according to the needs of the individual Indian, comforts of home, building homes, fences, irrigation, or whatever would be necessary for each person. Some who have good hay land would invest in cattle; whatever might best fit the needs of the particular person.

Mr. Stalker: Do those Indians have difficulty in making a living?

Mr. Walker: Yes.

Mr. Stalker: They can not make a comfortable living under present conditions?

Mr. Walker: They can not do any more than just meet daily expenses. That is all I am doing. For the basis of this request here they have a great asset, and to get it all in one bunch would put them in a position to invest this money, by each and every one of the Klamath Indians; but at present we may find ourselves down the river with no oars, floating down; that is the size of it. The same thing applies to irrigation matters, and everything handled by the Department of the Interior. It is just drifting along. We find under the act of Congress that the Secretary is authorized to sell timber on all reservations throughout the United States, for the benefit of the Indians, and I see nothing in this transaction where we derive any direct benefit. We do receive indirect benefit in maintaining the reservation, and they hire so many men to take care of the forestry; but there are expenses for things that are not necessary. We feel that our money should be expended just the same as any firm or corporation expends the money for things from which it expects to bring a return.

---

[2] *Gale Hamilton Stalker* (1889–1985), Republican congressman from Elmira, New York.

Mr. Stalker: Do you think it would be safer as an experiment to give them part of this amount? Do you think it would be good business to give them $4,000 at one time, taking into consideration their business experience in financial matters?

Mr. Walker: I can not say much about that because we will have to take anything given to us, as we have for 50 or 60 years been taking what is given us by the Department of the Interior; and if we do not get anything in this Congress we will have to continue to take that. We are not getting anything as it is, according to the amount of money handled, creating from time to time new bureaus, new positions, and finding something new where they could expend the money. We are looking toward the closing up of our tribal relation and getting down to business, and we want to prepare ourselves to meet that time.

Statement of Charles S. Hood

Mr. Stalker: In what way do you represent this tribe?

Mr. Hood: I have credentials from the tribal and general council of the Klamath Indian Reservation.

Mr. Stalker: Are you an attorney?

Mr. Hood: I have been admitted to practice before the Interior Department. I hold a license for that, with the exception of the Patent Office.

Mr. Stalker: What is your business?

Mr. Hood: I am a real estate broker, and I am the local agent of the Northwestern Mutual Life Insurance Co. of Milwaukee, Wis. I am local agent of the Fidelity & Deposit Co. of Maryland. I have been in the insurance business for a number of years.

Mr. Stalker: Do you live on this reservation?

Mr. Hood: I do. . . . I am glad of this opportunity to say something in connection with this legislation for & benefit of the Klamaths embodied in H. R. 7351. To make my talk as brief as I possibly can, the department has been selling our tribal timber for the last eight or nine years, and from the time that the department has been managing these timber sales we have received very small direct benefit from the proceeds of the timber sales. I think within that time we have received direct benefits probably in the neighborhood of a fraction over $600 per capita. We received $300 at one time reimbursable. That money was invested in livestock for each allottee. Later on they paid us a per capita payment of $150; then at another time, $80, at another time, $75, and at another time, $50. While we have realized these amounts directly for the benefit of the allottee, we have been unable to get the exact amount of money that has accrued from the timber sales, up to the present time. We believe it must be somewhere in the neighborhood of $2,000,000, in round numbers, so that our people are dissatisfied with receiving such small benefit from this enormous amount of money that accumulates from year to year from the sales of timber on the reservation. Our people have been making pleas and petitions to the Interior Department to give them more assistance in the way of moneys, or that they could expend this money for their own benefit, in the things that would appeal to each and every allottee.

For these reasons we have asked the National Congress to assist us in formulating this legislation, which we are asking, to extend us a loan of $5,000,000, or more, if they see fit. We have tremendous assets on that reservation valued at in the neighborhood of twenty-five to thirty million dollars. A number of years ago the department appraised the total wealth of the reservation at about $30,000 to each allottee. This wealth up to the present time is only in name; but I should say we are worth $30,000 apiece.

The department has expended money from the timber sales year after year, or as fast as the money would accrue from the sales of the timber, without giving our people very much assistance. We, have on that reservation about 300 Indians who have been declared competent and capable of managing their own personal affairs and who are citizens of the United States. Even these people have been deprived of receiving any direct benefit from the proceeds of the timber sales.

We believe that the majority of the Indians on the Klamath are in a position to handle their own personal affairs. I believe that there are probably in the neighborhood of 300 other people who are competent, and able for the department to bestow competency upon, but, for various reasons, they have refused to ask to be declared citizens of the United States, for the reason that they will be denied even the right to handle their own personal assets due them from this reservation. They do not like the idea of going to work, and paying taxes on their property, and not to be entitled to receive their full share of the tribal estate.

We believe that the management extended to our people is absolutely wrong at the present time. It may have been a well arranged affair a number of years ago, to restrict the red man from exercising a share in the management of his personal estate—in the assets due him from the reservation—simply because he was considered incompetent; but at the present time we have some very intelligent people on the reservation, some, I would be safe in saying, are more enlightened than the present delegation that are here to-day.

With this money a number of people would be in the field to endeavor to better their condition by different studies. We have a young lady who went to San Francisco several years ago to have her voice trained to be a noted singer. She made wonderful strides in that matter, but financial difficulties were an obstruction to her and she had to give it up. Last year she took up the matter with the Interior Department of trying to get a reimbursable loan from the department for the purpose of pursuing her studies in vocal music, but no arrangement could be made whereby she would be granted any of the tribal money to better her condition. There are others in that same predicament. There is no doubt that we are badly in need of this financial assistance. We have many young people on the reservation who would like to invest in the handling of livestock so that they could derive some means whereby they could better their condition in that way. But instead of that the department has expended a greater portion of the money derived from these timber sales for administrative purposes. I think the record shows here that the department has been expending something over $200,000 of the tribal funds for administrative purposes. We were also told that they could [not] expend more than this without congressional legislation; so that it puts us in a very poor condition, at the present time in the way of deriving direct benefit from the sales of our timber.

Afterword:
The Pueblos Protest
the Bursum Bill, 1922

For Native Americans, no less than for other people in the United States, the 1920s marked a new chapter in their relationship to the American political arena. The Senate's refusal to ratify the Treaty of Versailles in 1919 and the electorate's overwhelming repudiation of the Democrats the following year spelled the end of an era of government activism on behalf of workers and small-business owners. The 1919 race riots in Chicago and elsewhere in the North, and the rising congressional sentiment in favor of immigration restriction, also signaled the onset of a period when racist ideas and practices would be a national commonplace. Already under assault by allotting agents, missionaries, and paternalistic educators, Indian leaders could identify few in government who might sympathize with them or help them alter the course of federal action.

Indian people had rarely benefited from Progressive legislation — the reformers' energies had largely been directed toward gaining access to tribal resources and preparing Native people for menial employment — but the 1920s raised the specter of something even more destructive than allotment or inadequate education: public indifference. Increases in spending for Indian health, which had begun during the Wilson administration and which promised to extend public health services to most reservations, ended with the declaration of war and were not restored with the peace. Shocking rates of tuberculosis and trachoma infection, unmatched levels of infant mortality, and the lowest life expectancy figures in the country continued throughout the decade.

The pace of allotment slowed only because most arable reservations had already been divided; for those who held allotments, the iron arithmetic of leasing and land sales tore away at what little wealth remained in Native hands. Once landowners leased their property to outsiders, they fell into dependent relationships that made it virtually impossible for the Natives to acquire the tools and training necessary to operate their own farms. As time passed, landowners died and their property was divided among their children. These children could not make any productive use of their parcels other than continuing to lease the entire farm or ranch to outsiders.

With the stagnation in federal funding, Indian education continued to emphasize menial vocational skills and "lessons" such as cooking, gardening, and maintenance work, all of which did little more than train children to maintain the boarding schools where they were imprisoned. The closure of the famous Carlisle Indian Industrial School in 1918—its facilities were returned to the army to support the war effort—was symbolic of this shift. Despite its harsh conditions and regimented way of life, Carlisle had represented a national commitment to Indian "uplift" and a link to the idealism of the Christian reformers who had helped found it in 1879. Its closing shifted attention to local schools with modest goals and little federal oversight.

But the 1920s were not simply a time of suffering and stagnation. For American Indian leaders, the decades since Simon Pokagon had condemned the celebration of the Columbus voyages in 1893 had provided dozens of opportunities to talk back to officials claiming to embody the forces of civilization. These Native Americans had explained that government schools did not always promote "education" and that Christianity was not the only pathway to religious truth. Government officials were human, these native leaders insisted; their actions and policies were not necessarily motivated by virtue. In debates over public issues throughout the early twentieth century, Indian leaders had spoken out again and again, piecing together in the process a much larger and more profound argument: "Civilization" would be defined by equity, freedom, respect for human dignity, and a commitment to democracy; it could not necessarily be equated with the actions of the United States.

The Indians' new language of protest was evident in a number of settings during the 1920s, but nowhere was it more dramatically on display than in New Mexico in the fall of 1922. On November 3, 121 delegates from nineteen Pueblo communities gathered at Santo Domingo (not far from Santa Fe) to discuss a bill being considered in Washington, D.C. Introduced by New Mexico's Republican senator Holm Bursum, the bill proposed to settle a series of long-standing land disputes between Pueblo communities and non-Indian squatters.

Bursum, a political ally of Interior Secretary Albert Fall (himself a former New Mexico senator), was widely believed to be sympathetic to
the squatters. He introduced his bill in July, but opposition to it did not
crystallize until it was brought to the Senate floor without a hearing in
September and then passed without debate.

The Pueblo opposition to the Bursum bill was intended to stop the
measure before it came to a vote in the House of Representatives. The
November meeting was timed to produce a statement of protest prior
to the next congressional session. It was also planned in consultation
with a new group of non-Indian allies who promised to publicize the
Pueblo message in every corner of the United States. As the Pueblo
land issue was being debated in New Mexico in the years immediately
before World War I, members of the growing artists and writers'
colonies in Santa Fe and Taos had allied themselves with the tribal
leaders, who worried publicly that local politicians were overly sympathetic to constituents who had settled in disputed areas. Interest on
the part of writers such as Mary Austin and the art patron Mabel
Dodge Luhan attracted the attention of the General Federation of
Women's Clubs, particularly the California leaders of that organization. The General Federation, acting through Stella Atwood, chairman
of the organization's Indian welfare committee, subsequently commis-
sioned a former New York City social worker, John Collier, to investi-
gate the situation. Collier was quickly persuaded that the Pueblo were
about to be cheated out of valuable property and he urged all who
would listen to support the Indian cause.

Although Collier later insisted that the Pueblo conference on
November 3–5 was the idea of local Indian leaders and not orches-
trated by him, he was quick to capitalize on the event and to distribute
the conference declaration to the press and the national membership
of the General Federation. The document was printed on the front
page of the *Santa Fe New Mexican* on November 6, and a summary
appeared in the *New York Times* the following day. As the protests
grew, congressional leaders scheduled hearings on the Bursum bill
for February 1923. This delay doomed the proposal. By the time the
hearings were completed, accusations of corruption and mismanage-
ment had forced Albert Fall to resign from the Interior Department,
and enough questions had been raised to persuade legislators that the
Pueblo had to be included in the drafting of any bill. In 1924 Bursum's
bill was replaced by a new proposal that had the support of Indian
leaders. This substitute, passed in early 1924, created the Pueblo
Lands Board, which would adjudicate all claims; the law also stipu-

lated that it would take a unanimous vote of the board to decide a case against a Pueblo community.

The following text of the conference declaration that eventually doomed the Bursum bill is taken from the *Santa Fe New Mexican,* for November 6, 1922.

An Appeal for Fair Play and the Preservation of Pueblo Life

November 5, 1922

We the undersigned representatives of the nineteen pueblos of New Mexico, assembled in council in Santo Domingo on November 5, 1922, appeal to the American people for fair play and justice and the protection of our pueblo life.

Pueblo Indians have always been self-supporting and have not been a burden on the government. We have lived in peace with our fellow Americans even while we have watched the gradual taking away of our lands and waters. Today, many of our pueblos have the use of less than one acre per capita of irrigated land, whereas in New Mexico twelve acres of irrigated land are considered necessary for a white man to live on. We have reached a point where we must either live or die.

Now we discover that the Senate passed a bill, called the Bursum Bill, which will complete our destruction, and that Congress and the American people have been told that we, the Indians, have asked for this legislation. This, we say, is not true. We were never given the chance of having anything to say or do about this bill. We have studied the bill over and found that this bill will deprive us of our happy life by taking away our lands and water and will destroy our Pueblo government and our customs which we have enjoyed for hundreds of years, and through which we have been able to be self-supporting and happy down to this day.

The bill will take away our self-respect and make us dependent on the government and force us into court to fight over and to settle things which we have always settled among ourselves without any cost to the government.

Santa Fe New Mexican, November 6, 1922: 1.

Before this bill passed the Senate we have trusted the government, and now we find that unless this bill is beaten, the government will betray our trust. We cannot understand why the Indian office and the lawyers who are paid by the government to defend our interests, and the Secretary of the Interior have deserted us and failed to protect us this time. The Pueblo officials have tried many times to obtain an explanation of this bill from officials of the Indian office and the attorneys of the government and have always been put off and even insulted, and on one occasion when a Pueblo Indian talked with that government attorney who drew this Bursum bill about the bill, he was told that he was "ungrateful" and "no good." Knowing that the bill was being framed, a delegation from Laguna, the largest pueblo, waited eleven hours for a chance to discuss it with the Commissioner of Indian Affairs at Albuquerque. At the end of this time, the commissioner granted ten minutes, in which he answered no questions that the Pueblos had come to ask.

After we failed to get an explanation from government officials who are supposed to help us, we have ourselves studied what this bill will do to our life and our land, and have come together today to make a move by which we can appeal to the American people.

The Pueblo, as is well known, existed in a civilized condition before the white man came to America. We have kept our old customs and lived in harmony with each other and with our fellow Americans.

This bill will destroy our common life and will rob us of everything which we hold dear, our lands, our customs, our traditions.

Are the American people willing to see this happen?

Questions for Consideration

12. Why would Charles Eastman tell his largely white readers that "Jesus was an Indian"?

13. From the testimony of Francis La Flesche and Fred Lookout, can you explain why the peyote ritual would have been so appealing to Indians in the early twentieth century?

CHAPTER 4

14. When Carlos Montezuma called for the abolition of the Bureau of Indian Affairs, was he abandoning or supporting his fellow Native Americans?

15. How does Arthur Parker's list of policy suggestions differ from Montezuma's proposal? Where do the two men agree?

16. In what ways do legal cases—like a suit for damages or the return of land—differ from arguments in favor of a new law or Indian Office regulation? Is it significant that legal cases are typically brought by tribes rather than by individuals?

CHAPTER 5

17. Is there a common complaint embodied in the cartoons published in the *Quarterly Journal*?

18. Modern historians often defend the Wild West shows because they offered Indian people a chance to be themselves and to escape the regulations of missionaries and Indian agents. What would Chauncey Yellow Robe say to such an argument?

19. Could the arguments in Arthur Parker's essay on racial inferiority be extended to African Americans? Why—or why not?

CHAPTER 6

20. How did the language of World War I—patriotism, support for democratic governments, opposition to tyranny—affect the writings of Indian activists?

21. If Woodrow Wilson had had the time or inclination to respond to Robert Yellowtail's speech on self-determination, what might he have said?

CHAPTER 7

22. What is the basic point of disagreement between the Ojibwe delegates in 1920 and the congressmen who listened to them? Is the difference one of policy or one of philosophy?

23. Why are there so many restrictions on the residents of Pine Ridge Reservation? Why is there so much leasing? Can the policy change?

24. Do the reservation leaders who speak out in chapter 7 have a different perspective than the educated columnists who wrote for the *Quarterly Journal*? How would you describe that difference?

AFTERWORD

25. In many ways a petition such as the one submitted by the Pueblo Indians in 1922 is the oldest form of organized protest. What made this petition so innovative and new?

Chronology of Important Events for Native Americans in the Progressive Era (1890–1928)

1890   The Sherman Anti-Trust Act passes Congress. The new law outlaws trusts and combinations that act "in restraint of trade."

Congress creates Oklahoma Territory out of "unassigned" lands in the western half of Indian Territory. A large portion of these lands had been opened to white settlement in 1889 in the first of the territory's "land rushes." Later rushes occurred in 1891, 1892, 1893, and 1895.

Sitting Bull is killed by Indian policemen in his cabin on the Standing Rock Reservation.

The massacre of Sioux Indians occurs at Wounded Knee, South Dakota. Charles Eastman, the physician at the Pine Ridge Agency, tends to the wounded and accompanies the burial party that visits the site.

1893   The World's Columbian Exposition opens in Chicago to commemorate the four hundredth anniversary of the Columbus voyages. Simon Pokagon delivers his "Red Man's Greeting."

1898   The United States fights a "splendid little war" against Spain. American forces invade Cuba and capture the Philippines. The United States acquires its first overseas colonies: Puerto Rico, Hawaii, and the Philippines.

Congress approves the Curtis Act, which provides for the allotment of Indian Territory reservations and the ultimate dissolution of tribal governments there.

1901   Theodore Roosevelt becomes president following the assassination of William McKinley.

1902   Oliver Wendell Holmes is appointed to the U.S. Supreme Court.

1903 The U.S. Supreme Court issues its decision in *Lone Wolf v. Hitch-cock,* declaring that Congress has the power to abrogate treaties with Indian tribes.

1905 Theodore Roosevelt, elected to a full term as president in November 1904, is inaugurated. Quanah Parker, Geronimo, and American Horse ride in his inaugural parade.

Representatives of the Five Civilized Tribes hold a constitutional convention to oppose Oklahoma statehood and propose admission of Indian Territory into the Union as the state of Sequoyah.

Alaska creates a segregated public school system. One set of schools is for whites and "civilized" mixed-bloods; the second set is for Alaskan Natives. This system remains in place until 1960.

1906 The Pure Food and Drug Act becomes law in response to Upton Sinclair's best-selling novel, *The Jungle,* published in January.

Congress approves the Burke Act, which amends the Dawes Severalty Act by allowing the Secretary of the Interior to issue fee-simple titles to Indians, thereby making their allotments subject to taxation and eligible for sale. Native Americans who acquire allotments but continue with "trust" titles continue with federal protection but are no longer declared U.S. citizens as they had been under the Dawes Act.

1907 Oklahoma becomes the forty-fifth state in the Union. Tribal governments in Indian Territory are terminated.

1908 William Howard Taft is elected president.

The U.S. Supreme Court establishes the principle of Indian rights to water in arid regions in *Winters v. U.S.*

1909 Geronimo, still held as a prisoner of war at Fort Sill, Oklahoma, dies of pneumonia. The Apache leader had ridden in Theodore Roosevelt's inaugural parade in 1905 and published his autobiography in 1907.

Chitto Harjo, leader of the Hickory Ground Creeks who refused to cooperate with the allotment of their territory or to recognize the dissolution of their tribal government, is killed in a shootout with U.S. marshals.

1910 Daniel Beard's "Sons of Daniel Boone" organization and Ernest Thompson Seton's "Woodcraft Indians" join James E. West, a Washington, D.C., attorney, to found the Boy Scouts of America. The Boy Scouts were founded in Great Britain by Lord Robert Baden-Powell. The Indian lore merit badge quickly became one of the most sought-after awards offered by the new group.

1911 A fire at the Triangle Shirtwaist Company, a sweatshop in New

York City, kills 146 workers and spurs both union-organizing efforts and labor reforms.

The Society of American Indians is organized in Columbus, Ohio.

The Black Hills Treaty Council is formed on the Cheyenne River Sioux Reservation for purposes of organizing a suit in the U.S. Court of Claims to recover damages from the 1877 seizure of the Black Hills.

1912 Theodore Roosevelt challenges President Taft for the Republican presidential nomination, then runs as the Progressive party candidate. Democrat Woodrow Wilson, governor of New Jersey, is elected.

Jim Thorpe (Sac and Fox) wins two gold medals at the Stockholm Olympics. One month later, Olympic officials demand the return of his medals because he had played semiprofessional baseball in 1909. The medals were reinstated in 1983, thirty years after Thorpe's death.

The Alaska Native Brotherhood is organized.

Francis La Flesche, an Omaha, is elected vice president of the American Anthropological Association.

1913 The Federal Reserve Act is approved. The new law creates a national system of twelve regional Federal Reserve banks.

1914 The Federal Trade Commission is created as part of Woodrow Wilson's effort to regulate competition in American industry.

1915 The Hopi, weary of tourists photographing their ceremonies, ban cameras from their villages.

1917 The United States enters World War I on the side of Great Britain, France, and Russia. Ten thousand Native Americans eventually serve in uniform.

Commissioner of Indian Affairs Cato Sells announces that the Indian birth rate exceeds the death rate; Indians are "no longer a dying race."

1918 World War I ends.

The Native American Church is incorporated in Oklahoma to promote Christian beliefs through "the peyote sacrament." Frank Eagle, a Ponca, is named the church's first president.

1919 The U.S. Senate refuses to ratify the Treaty of Versailles because of opposition to American membership in the new League of Nations.

The Eighteenth Amendment, outlawing the sale of alcoholic beverages, is ratified.

A worldwide influenza epidemic rages across the globe between October 1918 and April 1919. American Indians suffer disproportionately: More than 20 percent of Indian population (300,000) is afflicted; 2 percent of those—more than 6,000 people—die.

A bill granting citizenship to American Indian veterans of World War I becomes law.

1920 Warren G. Harding is elected president on a platform repudiating American involvement with the League of Nations and calling for a "return to normalcy." Women vote for the first time in presidential elections.

1921 Margaret Sanger founds the American Birth Control League, which is renamed Planned Parenthood in 1942.

Commissioner of Indian Affairs Charles Burke issues an order prohibiting Indians from participating in traditional dances that involve "self-torture, immoral relations between the sexes, the sacrificial destruction of clothing . . . the reckless giving away of property, the use of injurious drugs . . . and frequent and prolonged periods of celebration."

1922 The All-Pueblo Council calls on Congress to reject a proposal from New Mexico senator Holm Bursum that would ratify the land claims of settlers who had squatted illegally on Indian lands in the Rio Grande valley.

1923 Calvin Coolidge becomes president following the death of Warren Harding on August 2.

The Navajo Business Council is formed to negotiate mineral leases with corporate clients.

The American Indian Defense Association is formed.

The "Committee of One Hundred," appointed by the secretary of the interior to evaluate federal efforts in Indian affairs, meets in Washington, D.C.

1924 Calvin Coolidge is elected to a full presidential term.

Congress passes the Johnson-Reed Act, which greatly restricts immigration into the United States by creating national quotas that favor northern Europeans.

William Paul, a Tlingit graduate of the Carlisle Industrial Training School, is elected to the Alaska Territorial Legislature.

1928 Herbert Hoover is elected president. Charles Curtis, an enrolled member of the Kaw tribe, is elected vice president.

The Meriam Report on social conditions among American Indians is released. The report chronicles Indian poverty and ill-health, underscoring the failure of the Bureau of Indian Affairs' programs of allotment, education, and the suppression of traditional Native American culture.

Selected Bibliography

PRIMARY SOURCES

Eastman, Charles. *From the Deep Woods to Civilization.* 1916. Reprint. Lincoln: University of Nebraska Press, 1977.

——. *The Soul of an Indian and Other Writings from Ohiyesa.* 1911. Reprint. New York: New World Library, 1993.

La Flesche, Francis. *The Middle Five: Indian Schoolboys of the Omaha Tribe.* 1900. Reprint. Madison: University of Wisconsin Press, 1963.

Parker, Arthur Caswell. *Seneca Myths and Folk Tales.* Reprint of several previously published works. Lincoln: University of Nebraska Press, 1989.

Zitkala Ša, *Old Indian Legends.* 1901. Reprint. Lincoln: University of Nebraska Press, 1985.

——. *American Indian Stories.* 1921. Reprint. Lincoln: University of Nebraska Press, 1985.

BIOGRAPHIES AND GENERAL WORKS

Britten, Thomas A. *American Indians in World War I: At Home and at War.* Albuquerque: University of New Mexico Press, 1997.

Hagan, William T. *Quanah Parker, Comanche Chief.* Norman: University of Oklahoma Press, 1993.

Hertzberg, Hazel. *The Search for an American Indian Identity: Modern Pan-Indian Movements.* Syracuse, N.Y.: Syracuse University Press, 1971.

Hoxie, Frederick E. *A Final Promise: The Campaign to Assimilate the Indians, 1880–1920.* Lincoln: University of Nebraska Press, 1984.

Iverson, Peter. *Carlos Montezuma and the Changing World of American Indians.* Albuquerque: University of New Mexico Press, 1982.

Liberty, Margot, ed. *American Indian Intellectuals.* St. Paul: West Publishing, 1978.

McDonnell, Janet A. *The Dispossession of the American Indian, 1887–1934.* Bloomington: Indiana University Press, 1991.

Trigger, Bruce G., and Wilcomb E. Washburn. *The Cambridge History of the Native Peoples of the Americas.* Vol. 1 (North America), P. 2. New York: Cambridge University Press, 1996.

Wilson, Raymond. *Ohiyesa: Charles Eastman, Santee Sioux.* Urbana: University of Illinois Press, 1983.

EDUCATION OF NATIVE AMERICANS

Adams, David Wallace. *Education for Extinction: American Indians and the Boarding School Experience, 1750–1928.* Lawrence: University Press of Kansas, 1995.

Child, Brenda J. *Boarding School Seasons: American Indian Families, 1900–1940.* Lincoln: University of Nebraska Press, 1998.

Coleman, Michael C. *American Indian Children at School, 1850–1930.* Jackson: University Press of Mississippi, 1993.

Lomawaima, Tsianina. *They Called It Prairie Light: The Story of the Chilocco Indian School.* Lincoln: University of Nebraska Press, 1994.

McBeth, J. Sally. *Ethnic Identity and the Boarding School Experience of West-Central Oklahoma Indians.* Lanham, Md.: University Press of America, 1983.

Pratt, Richard Henry. *Battlefield and Classroom: Four Decades with the American Indian, 1867–1906.* Edited by Robert M. Utley. New Haven: Yale University Press, 1964.

Reyhner, Jon, and Jeanne Eder. *A History of Indian Education.* Billings: Eastern Montana College Press, 1989.

AMERICAN INDIAN RELIGION

Jorgensen, Joseph G. *The Sun Dance Religion: Power for the Powerless.* Chicago: University of Chicago Press, 1972.

Ruby, Robert H., and John A. Brown. *Dreamer Prophets of the Columbia Plateau: Smohalla and Skolaskin.* Norman: University of Oklahoma Press, 1989.

Steltenkamp, Michael F. *Black Elk: Holy Man of the Oglala.* Norman: University of Oklahoma Press, 1993.

Stewart, Omer C. *Peyote Religion: A History.* Norman: University of Oklahoma Press, 1987.

GOVERNMENT POLICY AND INDIAN LAW

Clark, Blue. *Lone Wolf v. Hitchcock: Treaty Rights and Indian Law at the End of the Nineteenth Century.* Lincoln: University of Nebraska Press, 1994.

Harring, Sidney L. *Crow Dog's Case: American Indian Sovereignty, Tribal Law, and United States Law in the Nineteenth Century.* New York: Cambridge University Press, 1994.

Lazarus, Edward. *Black Hills, White Justice: The Sioux Nation Versus the United States, 1775 to the Present.* New York: HarperCollins, 1991.

Prucha, Francis Paul. *The Great Father: The United States Government and the American Indians.* 2 vol. Lincoln: University of Nebraska Press, 1985.

AMERICAN INDIANS IN POPULAR CULTURE

Berkhofer, Robert. *White Man's Indian: Images of the American Indian from Columbus to the Present.* New York: Random House, 1979.

Deloria, Philip. *Playing Indian.* New Haven: Yale University Press, 1998.

Dilworth, Leah. *Imagining Indians in the Southwest: Persistent Visions of a Primitive Past.* Washington, D.C.: Smithsonian Institution Press, 1996.

Dippie, Brian. *The Vanishing American: White Attitudes and U.S. Indian Policy.* 1982. Reprint. Lawrence: University Press of Kansas, 1991.

Kilpatrick, Jacquelyn. *Celluloid Indians: Native Americans and Film.* Lincoln: University of Nebraska Press, 1999.

Moses, L. George. *Wild West Shows and the Images of American Indians, 1883–1933.* Albuquerque: University of New Mexico Press, 1996.

STUDIES OF INDIVIDUAL TRIBES

Debo, Angie. *And Still the Waters Run: The Betrayal of the Five Civilized Tribes.* 1940. Reprint. Princeton: Princeton University Press, 1991.

Gilman, Carolyn, and Mary Jane Schneider. *The Way to Independence: Memories of a Hidatsa Indian Family, 1840–1920.* St. Paul: Minnesota Historical Society Press, 1987.

Hagan, William T. *United States–Comanche Relations: The Reservation Years.* New Haven: Yale University Press, 1976.

Harmon, Alexandra. *Indians in the Making: Ethnic Relations and Indian Identities Around Puget Sound.* Berkeley: University of California Press, 1999.

Hoxie, Frederick E. *Parading through History: The Making of the Crow Nation in America, 1805–1935.* New York: Cambridge University Press, 1995.

Meyer, Melissa L. *The White Earth Tragedy: Ethnicity and Dispossession at a Minnesota Anishinaabe Reservation, 1889–1920.* Lincoln: University of Nebraska Press, 1994.

Index